BEING A
MATHEMATICIAN

Gayatri Kalra Sehgal is an accomplished artist. Educating young children, with an engaging dash of creativity, was a new dream for her. She has attended seminars, intensive workshops and exclusive courses on child development, curriculum design, effective communication, train the trainer, etc., helping her understand the specific requirements of children.

She has set up a Day Care Centre and two schools, respectively, first as the principal and later as a dean, and carefully designed the academic curricula in both roles. She has innovated and revolutionized the novel way of writing report cards called 'Child's Intelligence Profile'.

Presently, she conducts seminars for distinguished educators and creates awareness among parents of differently abled children. This workbook is an extensive collection of her experiences and vision to create global leaders for tomorrow. She has also authored *Winning Strategies for Parents, SUPER CHILD! Unlocking the Secrets of Working Memory, Being a Creative Genius: Mastering Activities That Inspire Creativity* and *Being a Brilliant Thinker: Mastering Intelligent Thinking Skills*.

SKILLS THAT BUILD

BEING A
MATHEMATICIAN

Mastering Secrets of Mental Math

Gayatri Kalra Sehgal

Published by
Rupa Publications India Pvt. Ltd 2019
7/16, Ansari Road, Daryaganj
New Delhi 110002

Sales Centres:

Allahabad Bengaluru Chennai
Hyderabad Jaipur Kathmandu
Kolkata Mumbai

Copyright © Gayatri Kalra Sehgal 2019

While every effort has been made to verify the authenticity of the
information contained in this book, the publisher and
the author are in no way liable for the use of the information
contained in this book.

All rights reserved.
No part of this publication may be reproduced, transmitted,
or stored in a retrieval system, in any form or by any means,
electronic, mechanical, photocopying, recording or otherwise,
without the prior permission of the publisher.

ISBN: 978-93-5333-482-6

First impression 2019

10 9 8 7 6 5 4 3 2 1

The moral right of the author has been asserted.

Printed by HT Media Ltd, Gr. Noida

This book is sold subject to the condition that it shall not,
by way of trade or otherwise, be lent, resold, hired out, or otherwise
circulated, without the publisher's prior consent, in any form of binding or
cover other than that in which it is published.

To my sons,

Divyamshu and Kuber

Contents

Foreword | *xi*

Introduction | 1

PHYSICAL LEARNING STYLE

Activity 1: Adding the Holes! | 29

Activity 2: Wall and Ball-doubling! | 32

Activity 3: Stand on the Odds and Sit on the Evens! | 34

Activity 4: Time Machine—The Hourglass! | 39

Activity 5: Yummy Fractions with Coconut Macarons! | 42

Activity 6: Fractions with Healthy Cheesy Balls! | 48

Activity 7: Division with Gooey Stuffed Apples! | 51

AUDITORY LEARNING STYLE

Activity 8: The Multiplication Song! | 57

Activity 9: Magic Multiplication with Building Blocks! | 60

Activity 10: Spot Your Dance Partner! | 65

VISUAL LEARNING STYLES

Activity 11: Goodness Me! Number 3! | 71

Activity 12: Number Hunt! | 73

Activity 13: Guess the Measure! | 75

Activity 14: Multiplication Hacks! | 78

Activity 15: Fast-track Car Race! | 85
Activity 16: Pictograph! | 89

VERBAL LEARNING STYLE

Activity 17: Rapid-fire Multiplication! | 95
Activity 18: Division with Building Blocks! | 98
Activity 19: Trip to the Bank! | 101

SOCIAL LEARNING STYLE

Activity 20: Odds and Evens! | 107
Activity 21: Expanded Form! | 110
Activity 22: Paper Dress! | 113
Activity 23: Multiplication Tunnel! | 117
Activity 24: Dice and Coins! | 120
Activity 25: Race without the Crown!
(4-digit Multiplication without Carrying-over) | 122
Activity 26: Race with the Crown!
(4-digit Multiplication with Carry-over) | 125
Activity 27: Garage Sales! | 130

SOLITARY LEARNING STYLE

Activity 28: Place Value Kit! | 137
Activity 29: Planning! | 142
Activity 30: Shopping Calculations with Calculator | 145
Activity 31: Working Model of a Clock! | 147

NATURALISTIC LEARNING STYLE

Activity 32: Sunny Sundials! | 153
Activity 33: Estimate the Distance! | 156

Activity 34: Probably Yes, Probably No! | 158

LOGICAL LEARNING SKILLS

Activity 35: Add with the Tic-Tac-Toe! | 169

Activity 36: Interesting Time Facts! | 173

Activity 37: Calendar Connections! | 181

Activity 38: Subtraction with Calendar Rings! | 184

Activity 39: Finding the Leap Year! | 187

Activity 40: Balance! | 190

Conclusion | 193
Acknowledgements | 195

Foreword

I feel fortunate to endorse the book *Being a Mathematician: Mastering Secrets of Mental Math* by Gayatri Kalra Sehgal.

Each child is different in a class and each one has his or her unique style of learning. There is only one teacher in a class and she or he has to adapt the teaching style to suit the majority of a class. Presently, there is a wide gap between the learning style of the student and the teaching style of the teacher, and this gap can be reduced by constant upgradation of teachers' professional development and by keeping abreast with the latest research in the specific domain.

In her book, Gayatri has gone through the developmental psychology of children and specifically brought out an important point that each child is unique, and so, the teaching methods should suit his or her level of learning style. She has stressed the importance of bridging the gap between teaching style and learning style.

Gayatri is passionate about child development, audiology, speech therapy, curriculum design and communication, and has done extensive research in teaching/learning methodologies. This book is a must-read for every teacher, educator, parent and those connected with education domain in any capacity.

I congratulate Gayatri for her highly fruitful efforts in bringing out this book and I strongly recommend every parent and teacher to read it.

Anshul B. Sharma
Chairman, Shastri Group of Institutes

Introduction

Has your child's grumpy look ever surprised you when you accidentally have given a little extra ice cream to the sibling?

I am sure you have seen your child frowning and glaring at you. You might have even heard them say, 'You have given him (or her) more!'

Such statements can be credited to the emerging understanding of mathematical thinking in the child! So, when you hear something similar to this the next time, take a deep breath and play your cards smartly!

Children are intelligent observers and resilient learners. They are capable of understanding numeracy and arithmetic at an early age.

As the child grows, he or she experiences and associates new information in the local environment to that already existing in their brain. When parents encourage open-ended mathematical conversations with the child, the newly acquired information gets enhanced and stored in his or her long-term memory to be used later. The child begins to make the language used for mathematics a part of his or her own understanding and feels confident while expressing himself or herself.

Mathematics is a multifarious subject and children have divergent thinking. Hence, the subject should not be taught as a stand-alone or 'compartmentalized' subject. It has to be learned throughout the day, carefully interwoven with key aspects of learning to enhance mathematical thinking.

2 Being a Mathematician

Use math to exercise, develop and enhance mathematical thinking.

Parents struggle with the giant syllabus in an academic session. What goes amiss is the focus on mathematical thinking, which should be introduced to the child along with other concepts during the academic year.

While playing outdoors with your child, expose him or her to the key concepts to enhance mathematical thinking in a diverse and stress-free manner. This way, the enormous syllabus will automatically fall in its place! Moreover, self-study at home instils the required confidence in the subject. Most schools revolve around the similar curricula, and yet may vary in the 'level of complexity'. They may add or remove a few topics, but it will largely depend on the Board of Education that the school follows and its geographical location. The books may get revised every year; the syllabi may differ, but the concepts, by and large, remain the same. The focus has to be on developing and enhancing mathematical thinking, which should be introduced through these concepts.

Going forward, I will give an insight into the concepts that the child is required to understand at each grade level. It will empower you to support the child such that it enhances and develops his or her capacity of mathematical thinking. Also, you will get to know how to introduce the child to various academic concepts in a fun setting without the child getting stressed.

In an academic year's syllabi, a child needs to *understand correctly, practise sufficiently, learn precisely and master the subjects.* A 6- to 8-year-old child will have to master over *150 different types of concepts each year only in mathematics, and that too, in less than 180 school days!*

Why are we in such a mighty hurry?

Introduction 3

Parents can refer to the following topics to be taught during the child's academic session.

Grade I (6 to 7 years)
1. Counting and names of numbers
2. Picture and number patterns
3. Sorting, ordering and comparing (with pictures and numbers)
4. Number facts
5. Addition
6. Subtraction
7. Estimation
8. Measurement of length
9. Money
10. Time
11. Calendar
12. Shapes—two and three dimensional
13. Spatial sense
14. Fractions
15. Pictorial representation of data

Grade II (7 to 8 years)
1. Counting and names of numbers
2. Number patterns
3. Sorting, ordering, comparing and classifying
4. Number facts
5. Addition—facts and properties
6. Subtraction—facts and properties
7. Multiplication
8. Division
9. Estimation and rounding
10. Measurement of length
11. Money

12. Time
13. Calendar
14. Mass
15. Capacity
16. Geometry
17. Logical reasoning
18. Probability
19. Data handling

Child Development and Academics

Development milestone is the approximate development maturity of a child at a given age.

Academic curricula are traditionally supposed to be based on the age-appropriate development milestones of a child. However, it is not true for all children, as every child has a unique graph of development.

Mentioned below are ten development milestones:

1. Physical development
2. Personal, social and emotional development
3. Communication development—listening and speaking
4. Language (grammar) and reading development
5. Handwriting development
6. Cognitive development
7. Mathematical development
8. Sensory development
9. Creative development
10. Self-help development

All the development milestones are interconnected and jointly lead to the holistic development of a child. If the child is lagging behind in class, it is time to examine the age-appropriate development milestones to understand if he or she needs your help.

Introduction

For our understanding, let us consider that the starting, or emerging, development milestone is zero and the achieved milestone for a child is 10. The learning pace of each child is unique. Hence, on a graph of zero to ten, all the milestones, at any given point in time, will never be at a particular number, it will always be in a 'range'. Let us understand this with an example.

A child's development of reading skill may be at 9 on the graph, but his or her social skills may be at 4. Thus, the child may feel under-confident when expressing his or her understanding about the subject.

Focus on the cause and not on the problem.

Let us understand with an example. If the child is asked to solve a word problem but he or she is unable to read and comprehend the question, we need to help them enhance their reading and comprehension skills. This will help them understand the question first and then solve the word problem.

However, when a curriculum is designed, it considers the milestones of children that cater to that particular segment of students who are at par with the 'developmental expectations'.

If you wish to take your child to a diverse level of understanding, first understand your child and then help him or her with mathematical thinking.

If the child is not following what is being taught, please reflect on the 'Mathematical Thinking Wheel' and identify the weak link. Once you identify the weak link, begin to work diligently from the weaker link so that the child is not under any kind of pressure.

If the child is lagging in learning any subject, go to the previous level of learning, look for difficulties and commence diligent work from there. But keep a positive approach towards the child during the process.

6 Being a Mathematician

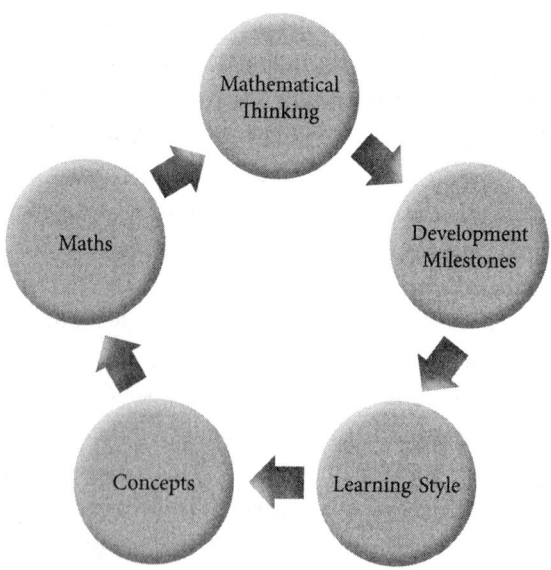

Learning Styles

All of us exercise our senses to absorb information. From the five senses, each of us exercises a predominant sense to absorb maximum information and store it as long-term memory in the brain. However, our education system barely provides adequate time and resources to create a learning experience enriched with resources to exercise mathematical thinking by using the five senses.

Going forward, the activities presented in this book will integrate the mathematical concepts taught in a different setting to enhance mathematical thinking for eight types of learners and their preferred learning styles.

1. Physical Learner
2. Auditory Learner

3. Visual Learner
4. Verbal Learner
5. Social Learner
6. Solitary Learner
7. Naturalistic Learner
8. Logical Learner

Sensory Area for Exercising Mathematical Thinking

There is a pressing need to design exploratory and experiential learning environment that has a rich assortment of resources, thus encouraging children to exercise their mathematical thinking as per their chosen time.

We know it is the most suitable way for everybody to absorb valuable information. However, what we do not know is why and how to create an environment that caters to it.

The 'Why'

Children perceive different things with the help of their sense organs. As the children begin to explore and discover things, they begin to relate the attributes associated with the objects. Hence, they begin to make more nerve connections and associations in the brain. They begin engaging in problem-solving and attempt to communicate their thoughts and thus, their mathematical thinking and language begin to develop considerably.

A rich and open-ended assortment of materials encourages children to participate in active learning and challenges them to extend their mathematical thinking.

The 'How'

Mentioned below is a list of 100 recyclable materials that are easily available in the surroundings for exercising and developing mathematical thinking.

8 Being a Mathematician

Remember to place them strategically (easy to access and at the child's eye level) and aesthetically for the learning surroundings to look inviting to the child.

100 Tools

Aquarium	Macaroni
Acorn	Magnets
Balloons	Mortar and Pestle
Bee hives	Mosaic squares
Bird nests	Mirrors
Bottles and bottle lids/covers	Musical instruments such as flutes, castanets, *ektara/tumbi*, tambourine, cymbals
Bottlebrushes	Nuts and nut shells
Brushes/toothbrushes	Organic colours—powders/liquids
Bubbles	Pasta
Buttons	Papers of different colours and textures
Canopy	Pebbles of different shapes, colours and sizes
CDs	Pens and pen caps
Ceramic tiles	Pencils and markers
Clay	Pets
Containers of different sizes and types	Pins—U pins, tack pins, push pins
Crayons	Pines
Composites	Pipes and pipe bends
Cones	Pulses
Coins	Paint
Cotton	Plants—natural plants and plant fibres

Cups	Play dough
Cushions	Potpourri
Dolls/doll houses	Rings of different shapes, colours and sizes
Dish soap foam	Sponges
Driftwood	Sand
Droppers	Scoopers
Earbuds	Seeds such as flax seeds and seed pods
Egg cartons	Shampoos and conditioners
Embroidery hoops	Shaving creams
Essential oils	Shells
Eye mask	Slime
Fabric—different colours and textures	Spray bottles
Food colour	Spices such as cinnamon, cloves
Feathers	Straws
Fairy lights	Sticks
Flour	Soil
Fur	Sequin
Glitter	Tepee tents
Hay	Toilet paper tubes (inner cardboard tubes)
Herbs	Tubes
Honey	Tyres
Honeycombs	Twigs
Ice cubes	Threads
Ice cream sticks	Walnut and almond shells
Kinetic sand	Water/sand wheels
Keys with locks	Water sprinklers

Being a Mathematician

Kitchen utensils	Wood
Jute	Wood shavings
Lamps for light	Wooden letters and shapes
Leaves—dry	Yarn

Children have significant mathematical understanding, but these 'understandings' fail to become their 'strengths'. Let us look at primary limiting factors that restrict the development of mathematical thinking in a children.

1. **Poor Foundation:** There are various factors responsible for a child's poor foundation when it comes to academics. Some of the possible reasons are not in your control while others can be carefully checked with conscious effort. Both reasons could arise when:
   - The next grade begins with a quick revision of the previous academic session. As the first term progresses, the concepts are gradually made more complex. For example, the picture addition in the next grade level will advance to addition with numbers, and later, the addition will develop with carrying-over sums, word problems, conversion sums and so on. The revision during the first term of the academic session is crucial, and I advise parents to take it seriously, as this practice has many benefits. Let us look at the potential benefits:
   - If the child has missed out on a topic in the previous class, it helps them to revise and practise the key topics all over again.
   - Revision during the first term of the academic session helps to bridge the learning gap that is created during the long and lazy holidays.
   - It also assists the teachers to recognize the 'level of

understanding of the child' and from where to commence work.

2. **Labels:** *Parents and facilitators need to remember that every child has his or her own pace of learning. We need to match our 'teaching pace' with the child's 'learning pace' and not vice versa.* Labels leave irreparable scars in a child's life. Passing snide remarks, using offensive language or getting disgusted and expressing through body language will hamper the child's confidence. You must stop all of that *at once*! We must sincerely appreciate the improvement made by the child in direct comparison to his or her own capabilities and not in comparison with the competencies of the other children.

3. **Teaching Malfunctions:** 'Teaching malfunction' is the incompetence of the facilitators to support the child in understanding the subject. Teaching malfunctions are:
   - The facilitator is ignorant about the child's level of understanding. Schools need to train the teachers and give them professional development to keep abreast with the latest research and the developments (R&Ds) in the field of education. Unfortunately, teachers are unequipped in 'Child Development' and 'Learning Styles' of the child and are clueless about what the child has accomplished or has missed out, which leads to complications for the child in the near future.

   If we presume that the child has achieved all the development milestones at par with his or her age, the next hurdle is the teacher's understanding about the child's learning style! The children are taught in large groups, which is the way the teachers are instructed to 'teach'! If the child is not taught in the way the child 'learns', the concepts taught might not be understood by him or her!

4. **Effective Communication Skills:** The facilitator lacks 'age-appropriate' effective communication skills to coach the child to get the best out of him or her. Children are given long and confusing instructions with multiple-step commands, which are not age-appropriate, and the child finds it difficult to comprehend. The child may not have the vocabulary developed enough to comprehend the instructions yet. Hence, the child, despite being age-appropriate and capable, gets confused.
5. **Boring Lesson Plans:** The lesson plans are not engaging enough to bring the child to the 'teaching moment'. It is a moment when the child absorbs every little detail the teacher teaches at that moment.
6. **Accountability for Learning Development:** Teachers are provided the present format for writing report cards by the schools. They are not held accountable to report the 'learning development' of the child. If a teacher is asked to credibly inform you 'how' they have concluded that the child has or has not learned a particular subject, they will provide you with score-based answers. But is that really enough to gauge the child's learning in the true sense?

The scores of the child are marked irrespective of the milestones achieved by them and in comparison to the other children in the classroom rather than in relation to the improvement shown by the child.

Parents must demand *more* from the education system! The school has to share the record of your child's development (or learnings) with you; it could be in the form of photographic evidence of the learning in progress.

Report cards, where the learnings were recorded on a scale from 0 to 100, started 100 years ago. Over a period of 100 years, everything has changed but our report cards!

Why?

It is easier for the schools to *not* provide professional development training to the teachers and simply hand over a report card of the child, without any accountability, to the 'not-so-demanding' parents.

Parents, this is a wake-up call! All the children do not report their understanding about the subject in the same way. Please reject the report cards with stars, smileys and those where the numbers are underlined in red ink presented to you by the schools.

Ask for more!

7. **Communicate to Navigate:** Adults use words such as 'right' or 'wrong' for the answers given by the child. Empower the child to communicate his or her thoughts. Then, carefully and lovingly navigate the child's thinking into the 'right' process. Our focus is to enhance 'mathematical thinking', and any harsh remark can hinder the thought processes. The child will withdraw or totally shut down the thought process if he or she is rebuked.

8. **Hurried Time to Think:** *The thinking of a child is spoon-fed! Give them time to think and come up with their own answers.* Remember that the child is trying; encourage him or her to take the risk of trying. If their answer does or does not match the expected answer, ask the child open-ended questions such as: why do you think this (the answer given by the child) is the correct answer? Is there any other possible answer to the same question?

9. **Offer Choices:** Offer choices to children. Invite them to choose the colour of worksheets and the handwriting instruments. Not all children like to use similar pens/pencils.

10. **Interfere or Intervene:** As we support the child, we need to understand the striking difference between the two words

'interfere' and 'intervene'. Many times, these two words are used interchangeably. However, the connotations of the two words are opposite. The word 'interfere' has a negative connotation and it means that you are poking your nose into the child's learnings and his or her thinking process. When you 'interfere' with their understanding, they are unable to form their unique opinions on the subject. Whereas, the word 'intervene' has a more positive connotation. When you 'intervene' in something, you are playing a more constructive role. You 'intervene' as a mentor, hold yourself back and encourage the child to take risks, allow him/her to be wrong. You intervene when it is appropriate to facilitate the learning in the right direction without interfering in the child's learnings.

Now, when it comes to Math, I want to emphasize on the fact that we focus on only developing math, which is only a subject, but we do not focus on developing mathematical thinking!

We need to use math as a tool to exercise, develop and enhance mathematical thinking and not vice versa.

Now that we have a clear understanding about the limitations a child faces in achieving their goals, let us look at the strategies that strengthen the holistic development of the child.

1. Have Faith in Your Child

We encourage children to draw and read for enjoyment, yet we never encourage them to enjoy mathematics! We teach mathematics as a regimented subject, done only in the way that has been taught. It is supposed to be done with speed in a given amount of time. If the child does not give the desired answer in the given time, he/she is disciplined. However, thankfully, drawing and reading are never taught to the child in the same way.

At this juncture, I would like to share an experience from

when I was 6 years old. As a child, I remember being an average student. No matter how much my mother helped me repeat and learn, I would goof up during the exams; though I tried my best. The turning point in my life came when my second-grade teacher told me, 'Good job, Gayatri! You have scored a 6 on 10. I am sure next time you will score a 10 on 10.' I felt the excitement rush through my veins. I could hear my heart beat. I went back home. I asked my father, 'Papa, will I ever score a 10 on 10 in Science?' He asked, 'Why not?' I looked at my father's face and saw that he believed in me.

Today, when I reflect upon my childhood, all I can remember is that my family loved me and they never gave up on me! Everybody has a 'turning point' in his or her life. Encourage your children in every possible way. Do not miss any opportunity of encouraging them in whichever field of study they choose to be. Had my father not supported in me, I would have been a failure for the rest of my life, believing I was good for nothing!

Have unflinching faith in your child. You have the magic wand for your little struggling angel.

I am reminded of yet another incident, which is relevant for the children who are different learners. My teachers told my parents that I 'daydream' and cannot concentrate in the classroom. A long list of complaints haunted me for the following week.

Today, when I think about this incident, I understand that I was an 'Intrapersonal-Kinesthetic' learner and to add to the 'problem', I had a creative bent of mind! In simple words, it meant that I had a different 'Learning Style' than the teacher's 'teaching style'. The teacher taught me in a way that helped all my class fellows but me. Since I had nothing else to do, I would build castles in the air.

The child in me learned a subject only when I was emotionally and physically involved with it. Sitting in a regimented classroom was a taxing thing for me. But as luck would have it, I had yet another turning point in my life.

That incident took place when I was staying in an army accommodation with my mother and my older brother. Our house was on the first floor and it had a parapet, which was like an extension of the garage on the ground floor. As a 6-years-old child, I used to slide on the parapet and jump onto the ground floor like a frog! I did hurt my ankle a couple of times though. Being kinaesthetic by nature, it did not make me think that I should stop doing that, instead it made me realize that I needed another way of jumping off the parapet!

The garden outside our house had a football goalpost, and one day, I was looking at people who had come to the garden for early-morning workouts. As a silently observing child, I saw one of them perform pull-ups.

I had my answer.

Thoughts began to race in my mind, and I did my calculations. I estimated the height or distance of the parapet from the ground and subtracted my own height to guess the impact with which I would land on the ground. That evening, I decided to hang from the parapet and land on the ground by releasing the grip. I landed on the ground safely!

Report cards could wait!

We need to remember that mathematical thinking is about *learning consistently and deeply,* and not just performing to get the *expected* scores.

Many mathematicians take time to think and think deeply. Hence, work at a comparatively slower pace than what we train our children at! Laurent Schwartz, a French mathematician, who won the Fields Medal in the year 1950, believed that 'Faster is not smarter.' Following is a very interesting excerpt from his

Introduction 17

autobiography, *A Mathematician Grappling with His Century* (2001).

> I was always deeply uncertain about my own intellectual capacity; I thought I was unintelligent. And it is true that I was, and still am, rather slow. I need time to seize things because I always need to understand them fully. Even when I was the first to answer the teacher's questions, I knew it was because they happened to be questions to which I already knew the answer. But if a new question arose, usually students who weren't as good as I was answered before me. Towards the end of the eleventh grade, I secretly thought of myself as stupid. I worried about this for a long time. Not only did I believe I was stupid, but I couldn't understand the contradiction between this stupidity and my good grades…At the end of the eleventh grade, I took the measure of the situation, and came to the conclusion that rapidity doesn't have a precise relation to intelligence. What is important is to deeply understand things and their relations to each other. This is where intelligence lies.

The excerpt gives us an insight into the thinking of a young mathematician who was made to believe by the society that there was something wrong about being 'slow'. But had the society looked at his 'thinking' as a capability, his struggles would have been much easier.

We all desire our children to be successful in life. I would suggest that you scratch the surface a little more to introspect on what that success means. Here, let us discuss the very frequently used term, 'success', which is not just relevant to Math but to life as well.

- What exactly is success?
- Is there a difference between success and achievement?
- What is the role that a teacher or a parent plays in helping the child to be successful?

When every little effort of the child is appreciated by the parent, it encourages them to convert their effort into a habit. This takes the child on the highway to success. *So why do we stop at success and not encourage children to achieve developed thinking skills?*

The four steps to achieve developed thinking skills are:

1. Encourage
2. Improve
3. Succeed
4. Achieve

Remember, anybody can be successful in life, but the people who 'achieve' have higher thinking skills, strive to gain deeper insight and focus on the true essence of learnings. They do not settle for less!

TIP: Make intelligent choices from the time when your child is young.

Your belief in your child will encourage them to feel valuable and will add to their confidence. It will encourage the child to proactively participate and transform his understanding into enduring strength.

Remember, the child will show the signs of self-belief by first breaking the mental barriers at home, where he or she is most comfortable, and then starting to absorb the information they receive. Then, the child will show signs of gaining confidence at home. Finally, the child will begin showing confidence within his/her friends' circle. You will be able to see the child move from one phase of learning to another, as you practise more and more with them.

Do not underestimate the child's capability to think mathematically. Also, do not impose misconceptions formed by the society onto your child and hamper his or her self-belief. On the contrary, believe in your child and make him or her believe in himself or herself.

A great teacher believes in the child and makes the child believe in his/her capabilities. They put in hard, focussed and consistent effort as a team. The teacher has faith in the child. Parents are the 'first' teachers of the child and should settle for nothing less than holistic learning.

2. Respect the Child's Needs

Many times, we as parents are so caught up in our own rush that we overlook and underestimate the requirements of our children. As a parent of two boys, when I put their perspective under the lens, I realized their requirements, which were genuine. For example, it is good to ask the children to prioritize and spread out their expenses over a period to manage their finances better. Involve them in the planning from the beginning and interact with them to make them mature and responsible 'planners'. It will make them bond with the family better. They will feel that they too are an integral part of the family's decisions and they are equally responsible for the well-being of the family. Nurture these roots.

3. Learning Pace, Not Teaching Pace

Each child has his/her learning pace—the pace at which the child is able to understand the information. Remember that the child is at the receiving end. Maintain your teaching pace with the child's learning pace and not vice-versa. Simplify information and slow down the speed of imparting knowledge to the child.

20 Being a Mathematician

Give adequate time to the child to absorb the information. If the child does go off the track, hold back. I know it is difficult, but we must intervene at the correct time. As you move ahead in helping your child, you will learn to wait and hold back in the process. Children will go wrong, and when they do go wrong, give them some time to rethink. They will eventually retrace their steps to where they started and then arrive at the right answer. In the process, they would have learned a lot more than your 'interference' in their learning could have taught.

Math Language to Express Mathematical Thinking

In this section, I would like to introduce the mathematical language that a child is expected to understand and speak at the age of 6. This section is indicative and should be used as a precursor to gauge the level of understanding in a child.

NOTE: The child may show an emerging level of language skills. However, we need to check if the child understands the word in the correct context.

Mentioned below is a list of words that a child at the age of 6 should know, understand and use in his/her daily conversation in the correct context:

Abacus, above, about, addition, adding, after, alike, answer, another, arrange, around, ascending	Backward, before, between, behind, below, big, bigger, biggest bottom	Calendar, circle, compare, complete, cone, cross out, cube curve, cylinder
Day, date, descending, diagonal, different, digits, direction, distance	Equal, estimate	False, far, few, find, first, fourth, fifth, from, fill

Graph, greater than	Half, heavy, height, hexagon, high, horizontal, hour	In, in front of, inside, into, is it, in all
Last, later, learn, length, less, less than, long, longer, longest, low, lower, lowest	Many, may, measure, might, minus, minute, missing, month, money, more than, much	Never, next to, not equal, number, numeral, number line
Octagon, ones, outside, oval	Past, present, picture, point	Quarter to, quarter past, quick, question
Rectangle, rhombus, round	Same, start, step, second, shape, share, short, skip counting, side ways, size, small, smaller, smallest, soon, sort, square, straight, subtract, sum, symbol, symmetrical	Take away, tall, tens, time, third, through, today, total, tomorrow, triangle, thin, thick, true, turn
Under, unequal	Vertical	Week, weight, whole, wide,
Year, yesterday	Zero	

Apart from the list of words, children face problems in understanding questions. They do not understand as to what is being asked. For example, they might confuse 'what' with 'how' in a question. So, we need to explain to the child the precise meaning of the questions mentioned below so that they can express their mathematical thinking correctly:

1. What
2. Where
3. When
4. Why

5. How/how many/how much
6. Is it
7. Compare
8. Fill in
9. Can
10. Discuss
11. Justify

- The games and activities help to add an element of fun to word recognition and language development in general. At this stage, the child will begin to observe and become more aware of signs, posters, T.V. commercials, and therefore, make the most of this opportunity where a child can read!
- Talk to them about what they see on their way back home from school. You will be able to gauge whether it is/is not exactly what they want to convey. If you feel that they are falling short of words for conveying what they intend to say, HOLD BACK! Prompt them once you are convinced they have genuinely tried to think of the correct words. Keep their minds engaged.
- Children do not know the names of various things in their surroundings. They may know the 'table' as 'table', but the teacher may call the table a 'desk'. Therefore, introduce vocabulary to the child as much as possible. Create a print-rich learning environment by placing words on different furniture and items in the house. Help them read the words during the day.
- Remember to add an element of fun in math games and activities to practise their numeracy skills as much as possible.
- Give them adequate support and build on their self-worth and confidence.

Math Tools

As we go from cover to cover doing the activities mentioned in this book, keep the following list of items handy, as it will invite children to explore and discover math in their surroundings. However, a resource list has been provided along with each activity that needs to be kept ready before the child begins an activity. Math tools must be placed aesthetically in the surroundings to promote learning.

Balance	Dominoes	Recyclable plastic bottles and bottle lids/covers
Baskets	Geoboards	Scales
Beads	Glue	Scissors
Bins	Jumbo paper clips	Shower curtain hooks
Blocks	Kitchen supplies—dishes, spoons, containers, pots	Sorting trays
Building blocks	Links	S-shaped hooks
Calendars	Measuring cups	Thermometer
Chains	Money	Timer/stopwatch
Clocks	Number cards	Washers and other little metal pieces
Cloth pegs	Number charts	White boards with markers
Counters	Paper of different textures and colours	Wood shavings
Craft sticks	Play dough	Yarn, ropes and threads, ribbons and strings
Dice	Playing cards	

Benefits of Incorporating Games and Activities

This book offers games and activities for children with specific objectives and helps them enhance their mathematical thinking. Each activity is governed by a specific set of rules, a coherent underlying structure and is designed to achieve these specific learning objectives. The below-mentioned learning objectives put together help to exercise and enhance mathematical thinking:

1. **Designing Purposeful Situations:** Situations that have specific learning objectives can be designed through games and activities for the application of skills to enhance mathematical thinking.
2. **Positive Attitude:** Activities help to radically reduce the fear of failure. It provides opportunities for building concepts and developing positive attitudes towards mathematical thinking.
3. **Increased Learning:** A child's ability to learn is enhanced when taught through interesting activities than those in regimented and structured learning surroundings. This is because of increased social interaction between children. They get opportunities to test intuitive ideas and implement problem-solving strategies.
4. **Diverse Levels:** Activities give the children opportunities to function at diverse levels of thinking. For example, in a group of children, one child might be dealing with the concept for the first time at an introductory stage; another child may be developing his/her understanding of the concept; and a third child may be forming a hypothesis and consolidating previously learned concepts.
5. **Provocations:** Activities can be used to provoke thinking to further explore a mathematical concept. The activities help them investigate the mathematical concepts and get a more

profound and concrete understanding of the topic being taught.
6. **Motivation:** As the children enjoy the activity, they tend to remain motivated to achieve, and learning happens by 'default'.
7. **Teamwork:** Activities have two or more players, and help the children bond as a team and work towards one objective.
8. **Taking Turns:** The players take turns and learn to wait patiently for their friends to finish.
9. **Competing:** Players try to achieve a 'winning' situation and enjoy victory.
10. **Decision-making:** During the game, the player decides about how to move or act at any given time.
11. **Completing the Task:** They usually have a distinct finishing point to reach in order to complete the game. The child has to strive hard to complete the game and this encourages persistence.
12. **Independence and Interdependence:** Children, during an activity, work independently of the teacher and learn how to be interdependent on their peers.
13. **Opportunity for an Ongoing Assessment:** While the child is involved in an activity, the thought process often becomes apparent through the actions and decisions he or she takes, giving the teacher the opportunity to carry out assessment of learning in a non-threatening surrounding.

Remember to Remember

1. Ensure the child is not allergic to any of the ingredients needed to carry out the exercises in this book.
2. Ensure food is not wasted and is used as a tool for learning.
3. When children are using sharp instruments for doing an activity, remember an adult's supervision is non-negotiable.

Yes, it could be without the child realizing that he or she is being monitored.

4. Children learn better when they are able to connect with the subject. Children, many a time, fail to relate to mathematics. To form the connection between the child and this book, I have introduced four characters—Sid, Guppy, Gugzee and Jugnu. Help the child connect with them by talking 'positively' about the four characters in your daily conversations.

5. Create situations around the four characters and encourage the child in resolving the situations. It will promote the skills required to develop mathematical thinking.

6. The activities designed will develop and enhance 'mathematical thinking' of the child by doing math, which runs parallel to the curricula of schools.

7. Parents do not settle for anything less than a 'genius' child, and why should you? But if you really want to achieve this with your child, move out of your comfort zone. Team up with your child. It is time to celebrate learning together!

51	52	53	54	55	56	57	58	59	60
41	42	43	44	45	46	47	48	49	50
31	32							39	40
21	22							29	30
11	12							19	20
1	2							9	10

Physical Learning Style

Activity–1

Adding the Holes!

RESOURCES REQUIRED

- A large cardboard box
- A child-safe craft knife
- A sheet of paper
- Pens and markers
- 3 lawn tennis balls

Getting Ready:

Keep aside an empty carton of a T.V. or a refrigerator for the activity.

How to Make:

1. Ask the children to take the carton and place it on the floor such that they are able to work on the broader side—the length of the carton.
2. Ask the children to draw five to six circles of different sizes on the carton with a marker.
3. Ask them to cut out the circles to make holes with the help of the child-safe craft knife.
4. Write a number above each hole—smaller the hole, higher should be the number.
5. Prop up the carton such that the holes face the players.

Being a Mathematician

How to Play:

1. Draw a line about four- to five-feet away from the carton and ask the players to line up.
2. Hand over three balls to each player.
3. Ask the players to throw the balls into the holes one at a time.
4. Elect a player to write the scores down.
5. Each time the ball passes through a hole, ask the player to add his or her scores and tell the total score to the scorekeeper to note down.
6. Once all the players have had their chance to through the balls, the one with the highest score is the winner.

Tickle the Thoughts:

1. Ask the children which hole they should target to score the highest.
2. Ask each child their total score.

> **Goals Achieved**
> - Better concept of addition
> - Improved mental maths
> - Exercised gross and fine motor skills
> - Enhanced creativity
> - Increased concentration span
> - Better concept of taking turns

Tick-tack Tips

1. To make the activity more complex, increase the distance from where the player throws the ball into the hole.
2. Also, as the players master the game, set a time limit for them to attain a score. Accuracy coupled with speed will help develop concentration.

Activity–2

Wall and Ball-doubling!

RESOURCES REQUIRED
- A wall
- A ball

Getting Ready:

Keep a small- or medium-sized, bouncy ball ready.

How to Play:

1. Divide the players into two teams—Team A and Team B. Ask the players of each team to form two rows. Give the ball to the first player of Team A and ask him or her to throw it at the wall, and ask the first player of Team B to catch the ball after it bounces off the wall.

2. Both teams are given 100 points each. Two points are subtracted when a player misses a catch. The next time the same team misses a catch, they will lose twice the number of points they lost the last time.

   For example, a player from Team A throws the ball at the wall and the player of Team B catches it. Team B scores 2 points. When the next player of Team A throws the ball at the wall again, and the player from Team B misses it, the team loses two points. The next time the Team B misses a

catch, four points will be subtracted. If they miss another catch, they will lose eight points and so forth.
3. The team that is able to catch the maximum throws is the winner.

Tickle the Thoughts:

1. Ask the children in how many times will their score become zero if they keep missing catches. (The score will never become zero, as the score will reduce in the following pattern—2, 4, 8, 16, 32 and 64. Twice of 64 is 128. Therefore, the team will have 36 points to begin the next round.)
2. Ask them what is meant by 'double or twice of a number'. Assign a number.

Goals Achieved
- Enhanced mental calculations
- Better concept of doubling of the digits
- Better concept of subtraction
- Enhanced gross motor skills

Tick-tack Tip
Another variation of the game could be that children start with 'zero' and double the score each time a team catches the ball. They will soon need your help to double the score.

Activity—3

Stand on the Odds and Sit on the Evens!

RESOURCES REQUIRED

Making the Dice:

- 2 cube-shaped cartons
- 8 white chart papers
- 1 black chart paper
- A glue

Floor space:

- A pair of child-safe scissors
- The Game
- 4 black tape rolls
- A printout of the game mentioned in the Tic-Tac Tips section.

Getting Ready:

Keep the required resources ready.

Method:

1. Ask the children to seal the two cube-shaped cartons from all sides using a tape.
2. Help them cut the white chart paper and wrap the cartons such that it covers all its sides. Glue the chart paper onto

Activity-3

the carton to secure it.

3. Ask them to cut the black chart paper into circles and glue them on all the six sides of the carton to make it look like a dice. The size of the circles should be large enough to be visible from the start and the finish points and small enough such that six circles fit on one side/face of the carton/dice.
4. Ask them if they can simply stick any number of circles on any side/face, or if there should be a pattern on a dice. Can they recreate the pattern without looking at a dice again?
5. The total number of circles on the opposite sides of the dice must be 7.

   For example, if the child sticks five dots on one face of the dice, then on the opposite (back) side/face the child must stick two dots to make the total 7.

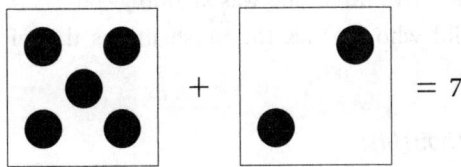

How to Play:

Give all the resources to the children.

1. Ask the children to stick the tape on the floor to create a replica of the game drawn on the paper.
2. Ask the children to draw squares such that they are large enough for the children to jump and stand inside them.

Let's Play:

1. Assign a number to each child; once they have created the game.
2. Ask the first player to take both dice and roll them one after

the other. If the total number of dots on the sides facing up is an even number, the child must jump to the square with an even number. He or she should sit on the floor. For example, if the child is standing at the start square and rolls 2 on one dice and 4 on the other, it totals to 6, which is an even number; the child jumps or moves to number six and sits in that square.

3. If the total number of dots on the sides of the dice facing up is an odd number, the child should jump to the next odd number. The child should stand on one foot inside the square and follow the instructions. For example, if the child is standing at number square 37; rolls the dice and gets 1 on each dice, the child moves 2 squares to 43. The 43rd square has the instruction 'Go back to 37!' and the child must go back to where he or she was standing—at 37.

4. The child who reaches the finish line is the winner of the game.

Tickle the Thoughts:

1. Ask the children how many circles they need to cut such that all the six sides of the carton/dice have right number of dots.
2. Ask them to count the dots mentally. (They will require 21 circles/dots for each carton!)
3. How many dots will they require for two dice?

> **Goals Achieved**
> - Improved thinking skills
> - Enhanced reasoning abilities
> - Exercised motor skills
> - Increased creativity
> - Promotes crossing the mid-line of the body

Stand on the Odds and Sit on the Evens!

START		37	38	43 Go back to 37		77	80	88		158	167	170
2		33 Jump to 38		44		76		91		151		171
3		26		45		75		97		149		179
4		24		48		73		98		138		180
6		22		53		72		99		137		188
7		19		55		69		100		133		190
9		14		58		65		101		128		198
10	11	13		60	61	64		109	113 Go to FINISH	119		FINISH

The above-mentioned picture has odd and even numbers in ascending order. The children need to draw this game on the floor with the help of black tape. Parents and teachers may change the numbers as per their requirements.

To make the game more challenging, you may specify what the child must do inside the squares drawn on the floor:

1. Stand on 1 foot, squat, sit like a frog and hop from one box to the other.
2. Say the multiplication table of that number before they move to the next square.
3. Spell out the number name of the next number.
4. Sing a song before moving to the next number.
5. Go and collect pebbles from the garden matching the next number.

Being a Mathematician

Tick-tack Tip

Children can make a dice using the template mentioned below. Ask them to draw the template on the chart paper keeping the measurements of a cube in mind.

Activity—4

Time Machine—The Hourglass!

RESOURCES REQUIRED

- 2 plastic bottles
- A pair of child-safe scissors
- A glue gun
- 100 g of salt
- 100 g of sand
- A marker
- A safety pin
- 1 corrugated sheet
- A digital watch

Getting Ready:

Find two identical transparent recyclable plastic bottles for making the hourglass.

Method:

1. Ask the children to take the two plastic bottles and peel off any labels.
2. Now, help then to mark and cut the bottle as shown in the picture.
3. Then, ask them to place the cut bottles on the corrugated sheet, and mark the circumference of the bottle. Tell them to

Being a Mathematician

cut the marked circles on the corrugated sheet.

4. Ask them to keep the bottle caps on. Using a safety pin, help them make holes at the centre of the caps of both bottles so that the salt/sand falls through them.
5. Now, help them to use the glue gun and stick the two caps together such that the holes in them are aligned.
6. Then, ask the children to put different materials into their hourglasses.
7. Ask them to stick the cut out circles from the corrugated sheet at the top and bottom of the apparatus, as shown in this picture, to check if it works. Encourage them to use salt or sand to test the apparatus. The hourglass is now ready.

How to Play:

1. Introduce a digital watch to the children.
2. Invert the hourglass and ask the children to record the time taken by the entire salt or sand to fall through the holes into the base of the hourglass.
3. Allow each child to invert the hourglass and record the time on a paper.

Mentioned below is a table for the children to record their observations. You can change the contents and the order of marking the contents as per the requirements.

Content in the hourglass	Time taken for the contents to fall through	Ranking
Salt		
Sand		
Sugar		

Flour		
Glitter		
Water		
Glue		

Tickle the Thoughts:

1. Ask the children what would happen if they put stones or water in the hourglass instead of salt.
2. Ask the children to carry their school bags from one place to the other within a decided time.
3. Ask them to record the time on the digital watch, while they are doing an activity.
4. Encourage them to talk about their observations from their recordings.

Goals Achieved
- Better understanding of the concept of time
- Exercised fine motor skills
- Better able to follow multiple-step instructions
- Enhanced communication skills
- Promotes data-handling abilities

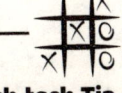

Tick-tack Tip

Children may decorate the hourglass with ribbons and paint the corrugated sheets to make it look neat.

Activity—5

Yummy Fractions with Coconut Macarons!

RESOURCES REQUIRED

For the Macrons:

- 1 cup (as a standard measure)
- 2 cups of desiccated coconut
- 1 cup of castor sugar
- 2 tablespoons cornflour
- 2 teaspoons cooking oil
- A pinch of salt
- 2 eggs
- 1 baking paper
- 1 chart paper

For the Icing:

- 2 egg whites
- 2 teaspoons of lemon juice
- 3 cups of icing sugar, sifted
- 2 food colour
- 2 ziploc bags

Getting Ready:

1. Let the ingredients be in the shopping bags and ask the children to pull them out from the packets.

Activity-5   43

2. If castor sugar is not available, grind a cup of sugar and keep it ready before children begin to bake.

NOTE: Ensure that the child is not allergic to any ingredients used to make these macarons.

Method:

Cooking Time: *20 to 25 minutes*
Servings: *About 24 macarons*

1. Ask the children to measure all the dry ingredients using the measuring cup and keep them in separate bowls.
2. Ask them to pour all the dry ingredients into a mixing bowl and mix them well.
3. Help them to break the eggs into another bowl and beat them until they turn frothy. Pour this mixture into the dry ingredients and mix to form a uniform paste.
4. Now, help them to grease the baking tray with cooking oil and cover the tray with a baking paper to avoid the macarons sticking to the tray.
5. Ask the children to place a teaspoon full of the mixture on the trays.
6. Ask them to leave enough room for the macarons to spread.
7. Under your supervision, help the children to bake the macarons at 150°C (300°F) for 15 to 20 minutes into a pre-heated oven or OTG.
8. Remind the children to wear mittens before removing the hot tray from the oven.
9. Allow the macarons to cool.

Recipe for Icing:

Cooking Time: *5 to 10 minutes*

Servings: *Makes 100 grams of icing*

1. Help the children to separate the egg yolk from the egg white.
2. Ask the children to add the lemon juice to the egg whites and whisk the mixture until combined.
3. Gradually add in sifted icing sugar and whisk for 5 minutes to form soft peaks.
4. Ask the children to divide the icing into halves and add different food colours to each. Fold the mixture until the colour is completely combined.
5. Use one colour icing for drawing the 'lines' of the fractions on the macarons and the other colour to fill in the fractions.
6. For drawing the fractions on the icing, put the icing in a ziploc bag and snip the corner to make a tiny hole. Their icing bag is ready now.
7. The icing is ready to pipe onto macarons, cookies or cakes.

How to Play:

1. Then, ask them to draw a number line on a chart paper. Divide the line into nine parts and number them 0–8.
2. Now, tell them to write down the fractions for each number on the line, i.e. 1 becomes 1/8, 2 become 2/8, and so on. Place a macaron under each fraction.
3. Ask the children to draw the lines on the macarons with the icing such that the circle is divided into 8 fractions. Start from the centre. They should look like slices of a cake.
4. Fill up the fraction corresponding to that of the number line with the icing, i.e., fill only the first fraction on the macaron placed at 1/8, fill the first two fractions of the macaron placed at 2/8, and so on.
5. Help them to do addition and subtraction of fractions on the number line. For example:

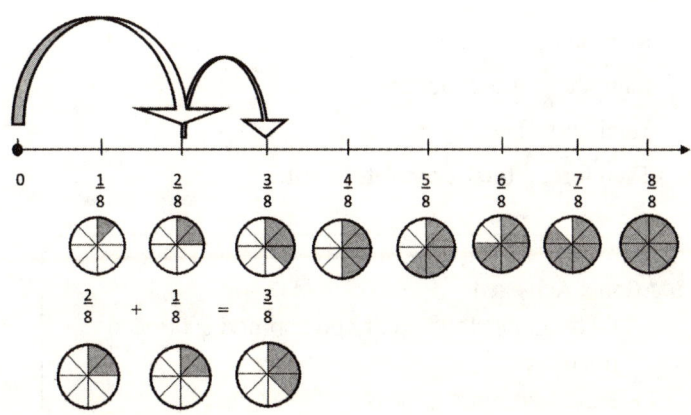

Tickle the Thoughts:

1. Ask the children what food items that they consume daily can be divided into fractions, such as idlis or chapattis. Ask them to cut a chapatti into half and ask them which portion they would like to eat.

2. Frame questions such as:

   Example 1:

   Rita read $\frac{1}{5}$ of a storybook at home and $\frac{3}{5}$ at school. How much did she read?

   Help them solve it:

   Portion of the storybook read at home $\frac{1}{5}$

   Portion of the storybook read at school $\frac{3}{5}$

   Total portion of the storybook she has read $\frac{1}{5} + \frac{3}{5} = \frac{4}{5}$

   Therefore, she has read $\frac{4}{5}$ of the storybook.

   Example 2:

   Raju ate $\frac{2}{8}$ of his chocolate. How much is left, if he had $\frac{5}{8}$ of the chocolate to begin with?

Raju had $\frac{5}{8}$ of a chocolate

Raju ate $\frac{2}{8}$ of a chocolate

Total chocolate left = $\frac{5}{8} - \frac{2}{8} = \frac{3}{8}$

Therefore, $\frac{3}{8}$ total chocolate is left.

Goals Achieved
- Better understanding of addition and subtraction of fractions
- Enhanced sensory skills
- Improved culinary skills

Tick-tack Tips

1. While the children are busy drawing the fractions, introduce math language to them.
2. Let us take the example: 1/2
   - The number above the line is called the numerator. It shows how many parts are taken from the whole. In this example, 1 is the numerator.
   - The line between is called the Division line or Bar.
   - The number below the division line is called the denominator. It shows how many equal parts the whole is divided into. In this case, it is 2.
3. If the denominators of the fractions are equal, the fraction with the larger numerator is bigger.
4. If the numerators of the fractions are equal, then the fraction with the smaller denominator is bigger.

5. Bring in the concept of fractions in your daily conversations for the children to master them.
6. You can store the icing in an airtight container, as the icing tends to harden when it comes in contact with air.
7. Children can use noodles to make the number lines too.
8. Ensure that food is not wasted.

Activity–6

Fractions with Healthy Cheesy Balls!

RESOURCES REQUIRED

- 1 cup (as a standard measure)
- 1 tablespoon of butter
- $1^{1}/_{2}$ cups of self-rising flour
- 1 cup of instant oats
- 1 cup of milk
- 1 cup of cheddar cheese
- 1 bowl
- 1 grater
- OTG or oven

Getting Ready:

Keep the ingredients in their original packing and allow the children to open the packets and pull out the ingredients.

Method:

Cooking Time: 10 to 15 minutes
Servings: About 15 cheesy balls

1. Ask the children to measure the ingredients using the standard measuring cup.
2. Help them rub the butter into the flour to make crumbs.
3. Ask them to grate the cheese and add it to the butter and flour mix.

4. Tell them to mix the oats and milk into the prepared mixture to form a dough and roll it into small and equal-sized balls.
5. Ask them to place the balls on a microwave safe tray.
6. Help them to place the tray into a preheated OTG or oven and bake them at 200°C or 400°F.
7. Bake it until it turns golden brown. It usually takes about 10 to 15 minutes.
8. Serve them while they are still warm.

Tickle the Thoughts:

1. Ask them how much is 1 ½ cup of flour. Can they show it to you using the cup?
2. Ask them to show you how much is 1 ¾ cups of flour.
3. What is meant by ½ a cup?
4. Using the cheesy balls make word problems such as:
   - Place five cheesy balls in front of the child and ask him or her to eat only 1/5 of the cheesy balls!
   They might nag and demand a few more cheesy balls. Offer them another cheesy ball and ask them to eat only ½!

Goals Achieved
- Better understanding about the concept of fractions
- Improved culinary skills
- Promotes messy play
- Enhanced sensory skills

50 Being a Mathematician

Tick-tack Tip

1. Introduce the concept of 'equivalent fractions' to the children by cutting the equal-sized cheesy balls into equal sizes as such.

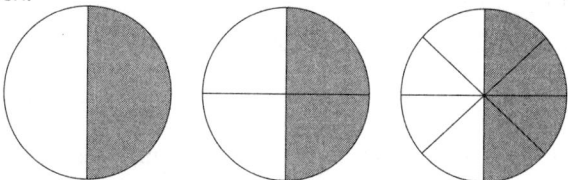

All the cheesy balls are of the same size. The shaded portions in each cheesy ball, in the figure above, are also equal:

$$\frac{1}{2} = \frac{2}{4} = \frac{4}{8}$$

Activity–7

Division with Gooey Stuffed Apples!

RESOURCES REQUIRED

- Dry fruits the child relishes
- 250 g of deseeded dates
- 6 apples
- 1 apple corer (refer to the given image)
- 100 g of honey

Getting Ready:

Keep the resources washed and ready for use.

NOTE: Ensure that the children are not allergic to the ingredients.

Method:

Cooking Time: 10 to 15 minutes
Servings: 6

Preparing the Apples:

Ask the children to take the washed apples and carefully remove the core with the help of the apple corer. Make sure that the children don't pass the corer through the apple and make a hole in it. Help them to press the corer

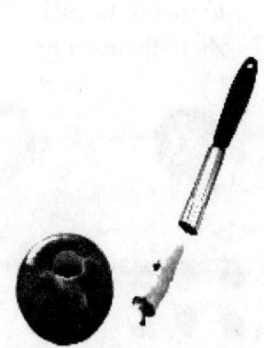

such that the base of the apple remains intact and all the seeds are scooped out. This will help the children press the delicious filling into the apple.

Preparing the Filling:

1. Ask the children to remove the deseeded dates from the packet, knead and loosen them well with their hands.
2. Help the children to put the dry fruits in the blender and blend them for a few seconds to turn them into a powder. Children may pound the dry fruits and break them into smaller pieces too.
3. Next, ask them to mix the dates and the dry fruits and knead them well. The gooey mix is now ready to be pressed into the core of the apples.
4. Ask the children to stuff the core well such that on cutting the apple, the mix is also sliced.
5. Now, let the children pour honey over the apples so that it trickles down the sides.
6. The math class is ready to do division with the 'Gooey Stuffed Apples!'
7. Children may slice an apple and share the slices with their friends. Frame questions such as: Sid has 6 apples. He wants to give 2 to each of his friends. How many friends can he share them with?

Activity-7 53

Tickle the Thoughts:
1. Ask them what according to them is division—is it adding or taking away. Explain the answer.
2. What is multiplication—adding or taking away?

Goals Achieved
- Improved understanding about division facts
- Exercised fine motor skills
- Enhanced sensory skills
- Improved culinary skills
- Increased ability to share

Tick-tack Tip

Go on to introduce the short and long method of division to the child only once you have helped the child practise enough, and he or she feels confident about his or her knowledge.

51	52	53	54	55	56	57	58	59	60
41	42	43	44	45	46	47	48	49	50
31	32							39	40
21	22							29	30
11	12							19	20
1	2							9	10

Auditory Learning Style

Activity–8

The Multiplication Song!

RESOURCES REQUIRED
- Chart paper
- A set of 12 felt pens of different colours
- A scale

Getting Ready:

Draw the multiplication tables chart given on the following page on the chart paper.

How to Play:

1. Ask one child to recite the multiplication table. Begin with a small number. Sing the multiplication table in the tune of a nursery rhyme or a song, such as 'Row Row, Row Your Boat' for the table of 4. After the words 'Row, Row, Row Your Boat', continue singing the numbers in the same tune of the rhyme, but this time, instead of singing the rest of the lyrics of the rhyme substitute them with the numbers 4, 8, 12, 16.

2. If you try to sing the rhyme a couple of times, you will get the numbers in the desired tune.

   This is how it goes:

   Row, row, row your boat 4, 8, 12, 16, 20, 24, 28 and 32, 36 and 40.

Being a Mathematician

- 'London Bridge is Falling Down' for the table of 6

This is how it goes:

London bridge is falling down 6, 12, 18, 24, 30, 36, 42 and 48, 54 and 60.

While the singer is singing the rhyme, ask another child to point out the answers in the Multiplication Table drawn on the chart paper.

3. Add some music by clapping or gently tapping on the table.

Multiplication Table

Columns

	X	0	1	2	3	4	5	6	7	8	9	10
	0	0	0	0	0	0	0	0	0	0	0	0
	1	0	1	2	3	4	5	6	7	8	9	10
	2	0	2	4	6	8	10	12	14	16	18	20
	3	0	3	6	9	12	15	18	21	24	27	30
Rows	4	0	4	8	12	16	20	24	28	32	36	40
	5	0	5	10	15	20	25	30	35	40	45	50
	6	0	6	12	18	24	30	36	42	48	54	60
	7	0	7	14	21	28	35	42	49	56	63	70
	8	0	8	16	24	32	40	48	56	64	72	80
	9	0	9	18	27	36	45	54	63	72	81	90
	10	0	10	20	30	40	50	60	70	80	90	100

Tickle the Thoughts:

1. Ask the children if they can think of a rhyme or a song to go with the table.
2. Allow them to experiment their singing skills by combining math and music.

Goals Achieved

- Promotes learning and revision of multiplication tables
- Enhances audio skills by incorporating 'math' into 'music'
- Promotes audio-visual recognition of the table

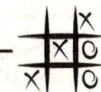

Tick-tack Tips

1. Instead of using a chart paper, children can make flash cards by cutting an A4-sized paper into small 6 to 8 chits. They can write the answers on each chit, such as 2 × 5 = 10. They can later dodge the tables to improve recall.
2. If the child gets stuck and is unable to recall the answer, hum the part of the rhyme that has the answers, and the child will come up with the answers.

Activity—9

Magic Multiplication with Building Blocks!

RESOURCES REQUIRED

- Building blocks
- 1 shoe lace

Getting Ready:

Write the multiplication table in the previous activity for the children to refer to while also singing it out loud.

Column

	X	0	1	2	3	4	5	6	7	8	9	10
	0	0	0	0	0	0	0	0	0	0	0	0
	1	0	1	2	3	4	5	6	7	8	9	10
	2	0	2	4	6	8	10	12	14	16	18	20
	3	0	3	6	9	12	15	18	21	24	27	30
Rows	4	0	4	8	12	16	20	24	28	32	36	40
	5	0	5	10	15	20	25	30	35	40	45	50
	6	0	6	12	18	24	30	36	42	48	54	60
	7	0	7	14	21	28	35	42	49	56	63	70
	8	0	8	16	24	32	40	48	56	64	72	80
	9	0	9	18	27	36	45	54	63	72	81	90
	10	0	10	20	30	40	50	60	70	80	90	100

Magic Multiplication Rules:

Explain the rules of magic multiplication to the children. Multiplication is adding the one number repeatedly. For example:

There are 3 groups of cupcakes with 2 cupcakes each.

On adding them repeatedly, we get 2 + 2 + 2 = 6

Repeated addition of the same number is called multiplication.

To further understand multiplication, help them with the following drill:

3 + 3 + 3 + 3 = ?	3 × 4 =
5 + 5 + 5 + 5 + 5 + 5 =	5 × 6 =
4 + 4 =	4 × 2 =
2 + 2 + 2 + 2 + 2 =	2 × 5 =

Method:

1. Ask the children to use a large rectangular piece of building blocks to form the base as shown in picture.
2. Ask the children to build equidistant 'buildings' of the same height. And number them 0–10.

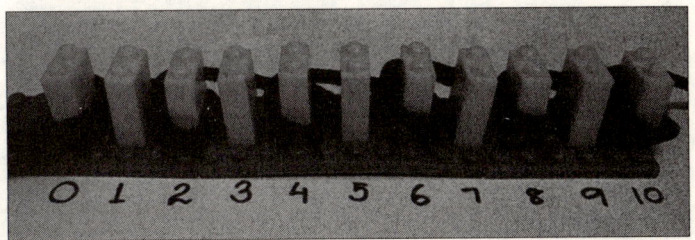

Being a Mathematician

How to Play:

1. Ask one child to recite the multiplication table. Begin with the more familiar ones. Remember to keep the mood light by adding some element of music and jokes.

   To multiply 2 by 5 or 2 × 5, wrap the shoe lace around the 'buildings', starting at zero, jump one number and tie it around the second number. Repeat the process five times.

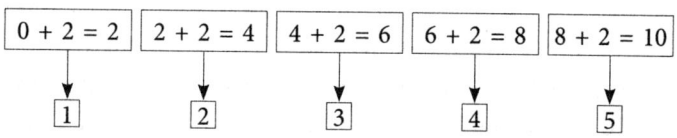

   Therefore, 2 × 5 = 10

2. Encourage the children to count the number of jumps to get to the answer.
3. Next, ask the children to check their answers on the Multiplication Table. To add some fun to it, you may name it MMT—Magic Multiplication Table!

Tickle the Thoughts:

1. Share the Multiplication Table with the child and ask him or her what is any number multiplied by 1?
2. What is 4 × 6 and 6 × 4. Why are they equal?
3. Can you use MMT to solve the sums given below?

3 × 6 =	4 × 4 =
1 × 9 =	7 × 8 =
5 × 4 =	9 × 2 =

Goals Achieved
- Improved multiplication speed
- Enhanced understanding about the multiplication facts
- Better able to follow multiple-step instructions
- Better ability to compare their answers to the ones given on MMT

Tick-tack Tips

1. Introduce three important terms of multiplication to the children. Let us use the 4 × 5 = 20 as an example to understand the following terms:
   - Multiplicand—The number to be multiplied is called the multiplicand. In the given example, 4 is the multiplicand.
   - Multiplier—The number that the multiplicand is multiplied by is called the multiplier. In the given example, the multiplier is 5.
   - Product—The answer to the multiplication is called the product. In the given example, the product is 20.

2. Multiplication facts:
   - Any number multiplied by 1 is the number itself.

     4 × 1 = 4, 8 × 1 = 8
   - Any number multiplied by two will give an even number as an answer.

     4 × 2 = 8, 5 × 2 = 10
   - Any number multiplied by 5 will give an answer ending in 0 or 5.

     2 × 5 = 10 (ending with 0) or 7 × 5 = 35 (ending with 5)

Being a Mathematician

- Any number multiplied by 10 will always give an answer ending in 0.

  $5 \times 10 = 50, 8 \times 10 = 80$

3. Just as in addition, even if the order of the numbers is changed, the answer remains the same. Similarly, in multiplication, the answer remains the same even if the order of the numbers of the multiplicand and the multiplier is changed. For example, the answer for the following example remains 28 even when the order of the numbers is interchanged:

   $4 \times 7 = 28$ and $7 \times 4 = 28$

Activity—10

Spot Your Dance Partner!

RESOURCES REQUIRED

- 4 chart papers
- Set of 12 felt pens of different colours
- Thread
- Worksheets
- A4-sized paper of 4 different colours
- 1 basket/tray

Getting Ready:

Keep a playlist ready for the children to dance to.

Method:

1. Ask the children to cut each chart paper into eight strips.
2. Ask them to write the multiplication sets on one strip and their corresponding answers on other strips.
3. Now, ask them to attach the thread at the corners of the paper strips such that the children can wear them on their chest like an identity card.

How to Play:

1. Ask them to spot their 'answer partners' and dance with them till the music is playing.

2. Stop the music; those who didn't find their partners during the dance are eliminated.
3. Each time someone is eliminated, ask the children to take off their strips. Urge them to shuffle the strips and distribute them among the children. They wear different strips for their partners to spot them. To make the game more and more challenging, reduce the duration of the music.
4. The remaining last pair at the end of the dance is the winner.
5. Parents and grandparents can also join in the dance at home to help them revise the multiplication tables.

Once children have had their share of fun, let's take multiplication to the next level:

Once Again—Getting Ready:

1. Ask the children to write the multiplication tables on the A4-sized sheet as mentioned in 'Tickle the Thoughts'.
2. Urge them to place the worksheets properly in a basket or a tray.
3. Next, ask them to choose the colour of the worksheets and the felt pens.

Tickle the Thoughts:

- Mentioned below are the multiplication facts: Any number multiplied by 1 is the number itself.
$$6 \times 1 = 6, 1 \times 6 = 6$$
- Any number multiplied by 2 will give an even number.
$$4 \times 2 = 8, 5 \times 2 = 10$$
- Any number multiplied by 5 will give a number ending in 0 or 5.
$$2 \times 5 = 10 \text{ (ending in 0) or } 5 \times 7 = 35 \text{ (ending in 5)}$$
- Any number multiplied by 10 will always give a number ending in 0.

Activity-10

$5 \times 10 = 50$, $15 \times 10 = 150$

- Simple facts about multiplication by 10, 100, 1000.

	Tth	Th	H	T	O	How to Write
8 × 10 = 8 tens				8	0	8 with 1 zero
8 × 100 = 8 hundreds			8	0	0	8 with 2 zeros
8 × 1000 = 8 thousands		8	0	0	0	8 with 3 zeros
7 × 20 = 7 × 2 tens = 14 tens			1	4	0	14 with 1 zero
7 × 200= 7 × 2 hundreds = 14 hundreds		1	4	0	0	14 with 2 zeros
7 × 2000= 7 × 2 thousands = 14 thousands	1	4	0	0	0	14 with 3 zeros

1. Just as in addition, if the order of the numbers is changed, the answer remains the same; in multiplication too, if the order of numbers are changed, the product will remain the same. Therefore, if the order of the multiplicand and the multiplier are rearranged, the answer remains the same. For example, the answer is 20 even when 4 and 5 are interchanged in 4 × 5 to form 5 × 4.

2. Ask the children which 'multiplication fact' applies for calculating the answers to match the balloons in the given picture.

Match the boxes with the balloons:

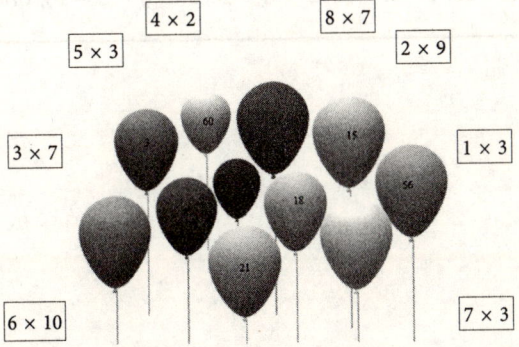

Being a Mathematician

🎯 Goals Achieved
- Enhanced retrieval of information
- Increased understanding about multiplication facts
- Better ability to recall answers by dodging the tables
- Improved social skills
- Enhanced gross motor skills

Tick-tack Tip

The balloon game can also be played with the children in a park/garden/classroom. All that you will require is to ask each child to blow/inflate a balloon and write a number with a marker on each balloon. Shuffle the balloons; ask them to choose a balloon of their favourite colour. Then, ask them to tell you the different multiplication tables that have the number written on the balloon. For example:

If the number written on the balloon is 18, the child needs to point out tables that have the product of the multiplicand and the multiplier as 18.

2 × 9 = 18, 9 × 2 = 18, 3 × 6 = 18 and 6 × 3 = 18, and so on.

Visual Learning Styles

Activity–11

Goodness Me! Number 3!

> **RESOURCES REQUIRED:**
> - A paper and a pencil
> - A clipboard
> - A floor mat

Getting Ready:

1. Fix a piece of paper on the clipboard.
2. Ask each player to draw columns and write their names at the top of each column.
3. Spread the mat and ask the players to sit on the mat in a circle.

How to Play:

1. Ask them to elect a player to keep scores.
2. Ask them to think of the total score that they must reach to be the winner. Tell them to select a number that is a multiple of 10, such as 100.
3. Then, assign a number to each player.
4. Players take turns to roll the dice on the mat.
5. A player scores only when the numbers show up in a pair of identical numbers when the dice is rolled. For example, two 1s, two 2s, and so on.
6. A pair of 2s scores 5 points.

Being a Mathematician

7. A pair of 6s scores 10 points.
8. A pair of 3s wipes out the player's past three scores.
9. The player to score the fastest predefined mark is the winner.

Tickle the Thoughts:

1. Ask your children if they can design a new game with the same rules but with a new set of numbers. Would they like to change the number from 3?
2. Ask them if they would like to change the rules of the same game. What will the new rules be?
3. Ask them to name the new game.

> ### Goals Achieved
> - Better concept of addition
> - Increased understanding of subtraction
> - Promotes mathematical thinking
> - Better concept of taking turns

Tick-tack Tips

1. A more moderate version of the game could be to begin with subtracting the last score instead of the last three scores. You may introduce this game with another name, such as Only Number 1!
2. To increase the level of complexity of this activity, have a bigger number for the total score, such as 500 instead of 100.
3. As they master the game, change addition and subtraction to multiplication and division.

Activity–12

Number Hunt!

RESOURCES REQUIRED
- A lot of time

Getting Ready:
Keep plenty of time in hand to play this game with the children.

How to Play:
1. Assign the responsibility of calling out numbers to one player.
2. Ask the other players to go around the house and look for items that represent the number that has been called out. For example, if the child calls out number 4, the other children should look for furniture with four legs.

Tickle the Thoughts:
1. Ask the children what other things can they think of to represent the number.
2. Ask them which number will a hanging curtain/a dot on the window/straight lines of the tile on the floor represent.

Goals Achieved

- Clarity in the concept of sorting, comparing and classifying
- Better understanding of number facts
- Enhanced investigating abilities

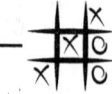

Tick-tack Tip

To increase the level of complexity of the game, choose a bigger number such as 200. It could be a book of 200 pages!

Activity–13

Guess the Measure!

RESOURCES REQUIRED

- Things to measure with, such as measuring jars, glasses, flower pot, weighing scale, etc.

Getting Ready:

1. Create an environment where children can find the required resources kept at various places.
2. Preferably, hide them at the child's eye level.

How to Play:

1. Ask the children to find things they want to measure in their surroundings. For example, they might want to measure the width, height and distance of the doorway of the house or fill up a bucket with sand using a mug.
2. Ask them to choose their preferred measuring scale. Let us suppose the child wants to measure sand in a bucket, and he or she chooses to use a mug to estimate the quantity of sand in the bucket.
3. First, ask them to guess how many mugs would fill up the bucket. Ask them to remember what they say. It is all right if they are wrong in the end. Next, ask them to fill up the mugs and begin pouring sand into the bucket.

4. Ask the child to count the number of mugs that fill up the bucket.
5. When the child has filled up 1/4th of the bucket, ask him or her if the bucket is half full or full empty.

Introduce Rounding Numbers:

- If 10 mugs of sand are needed to fill up the bucket and the total number of mugs poured into the bucket are 5, 6, 7, 8 or 9, the number must be 'rounded-up' to the nearest 10. On the contrary, if the number of mugs poured into the bucket are 0, 1, 2, 3 or 4, they must be 'rounded-down' to the nearest 10. For example, if a bucket needs 30 mugs of sand to fill up and the children have poured 27 mugs of sand into the bucket, it can be said that it is almost full and can be 'rounded-up' to the nearest 10—30. On the contrary, 24 is 'rounded down' to its nearest ten, which is 20.
- Although the results are slightly less accurate, their values are relatively close to what they originally are.

After the children have given their estimations, ask them to carry out their estimations to see how close they get to their pre-recorded estimations.

Tickle the Thoughts:

1. Ask the child if the mug is replaced with a jug, will the number of jugs required to fill up the bucket remain the same.
2. Keeping the measuring glass the same, change the contents in the bucket, such as sand, water, marbles, etc., and ask them about the item, which will weigh more or less and why.
3. Ask them how many blocks they will need to lay down to measure the width of the window.

4. Ask them how many marbles they will need to fill up the container.

> ### Goals Achieved
> - Promotes abstract thinking
> - Better understanding of the concept of estimation and rounding
> - Increased understanding about using the non-standard methods of measuring

> **Tick-tack Tip**
> Once they have finished estimating and rounding numbers with one item, use the same item but change its property. Ask them for the estimations again. Ask them the weight of the sand instead of the quantity, add water to sand and tickle the thoughts again.

Activity–14

Multiplication Hacks!

RESOURCES REQUIRED

- A paper
- A pencil

Getting Ready:

1. Give a paper to the children to write the tables.
2. If the number of children are too many, use a chart paper.

Clickety-click, How to Trick:

Making the Table of 7

Step 1:

1. Ask the children to draw a square with 3 rows and 3 columns as shown in the picture below:

Top Left Corner				Top Right Corner
	7	4	1	
	8	5	2	
	9	6	3	

2. Next, ask the children to write numbers from 1 to 9 in small squares from the top right corner, going down as indicated by the arrow.
3. Then, ask them to write numbers 4, 5 and 6, starting at the top-middle square and moving down.
4. Similarly, ask them to write 7, 8 and 9, starting at the top-left square and moving down.

Step 2:

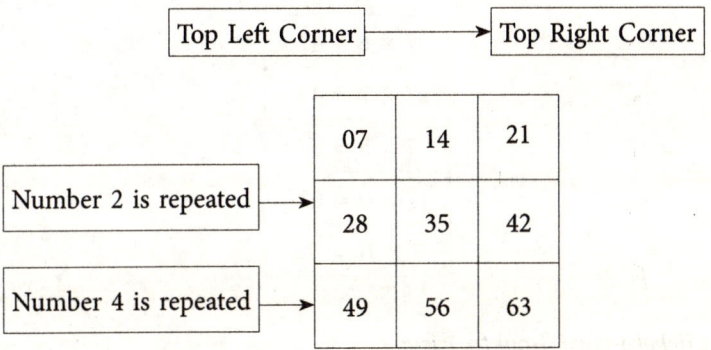

1. Ask the children to begin with 0 from the top-left corner of the square, moving from left to right. Urge them to write the numbers 'before' those written earlier. Therefore, in the first row, the numbers to be written are 0, 1 and 2, and the new numbers formed are 07, 14 and 21 in the top row.
2. In the second row, ask them to repeat the number that was written at the tens place in the last square of the previous row—2 in 21. Therefore, the first number of the second row is 28. Similarly, the digit at the tens place '4' in the number 42 is repeated in the third row. The number '4' is placed before the number '9' to make it 49.
3. The remaining numbers 5 and 6 will follow in the regular manner.

80 Being a Mathematician

4. The table of 7 is ready.
5. Ask the children to give it a go:

7 × 1 = 07
7 × 2 = 14
7 × 3 = 21
7 × 4 = 28
7 × 5 = 35
7 × 6 = 42
7 × 7 = 49
7 × 8 = 56
7 × 9 = 63
7 × 10 = 70

Clickety-click, How to Trick:

Help the children to write the table of '9' without mugging it up.

1. Ask the children to write the numbers 0–9 in a column on a sheet.
2. Then, ask them to repeat the process to make another column; only this time, they must begin writing the same set of numbers from the bottom to the top of the sheet.
3. Ask them to place both columns close to one another such that all the numbers in both columns are well aligned. Therefore, aligning and combining the first two numbers will give 09; aligning and combining to the next two numbers will give 18, and so on.

Activity-14   81

	Left Vertical		
9 × 1 = 09		0	9
9 × 2 = 18		1	8
9 × 3 = 27		2	7
9 × 4 = 36		3	6
9 × 5 = 45		4	5
9 × 6 = 54		5	4
9 × 7 = 63		6	3
9 × 8 = 72		7	2
9 × 9 = 81		8	1
9 × 10 = 90		9	0

Right Vertical

4. Once the table is ready, ask the children to verify the table.

Here is how:

The total of the two numbers such as 0 + 9 will always be equal to 9. Ensure that the left and the right verticals are aligned and placed exactly in front of each other.

Let us understand it with a few examples:

1 + 8 = 9
5 + 4 = 9
7 + 2 = 9

Yet another simple way to learn the table of 9 is by using the fingers.

82 Being a Mathematician

Clickety-click; How to Trick:

1. Ask the children to stretch out the hands and count their fingers, from 1 to 10, starting from the left thumb. (The children may use their right thumb as number 1 as well). Also, note that the little finger of the right hand, in this example has been counted as the sixth finger.
2. Then, explain the magic trick using the following example.
   Example 1:
   Ask them what is 9 × 7 = ?
   Then, ask them to curl their seventh finger.
   Now, ask them to count the fingers stretched out before the seventh one. The answer is 6.
3. Next, ask them to count the number of fingers stretched out after the seventh finger. The answer is 3.

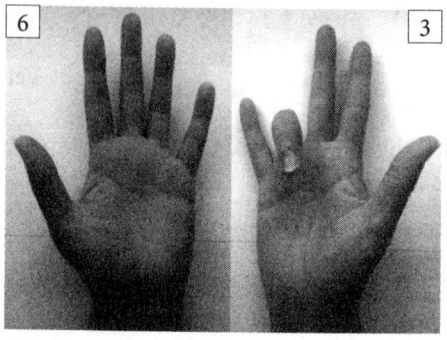

Hence, the answer to 9 × 7 = 63

Example 2:
Ask them what is 9 × 9 = ?
Then, ask them to curl their ninth finger. Now, ask them to count the number of fingers stretched out before the ninth finger; the answer is 8. Next, ask them to count the number of fingers that are stretched out after the ninth finger; the answer is 1.

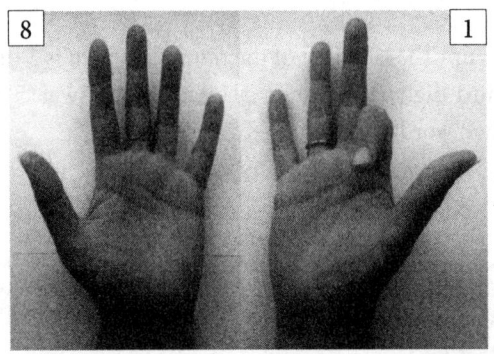

Therefore, 9 × 9 = 81

Now that they have learned the tricks, here is a technique that will give them a winning edge to multiply bigger numbers.

Example 1:

Multiply 11 with a single digit such as:

11 × 5 = ?

When we have to multiply any one-digit number—for instance, 5 here—with 11, simply repeat the number 5 twice to get the answer 55.

11 × 5 = 55

Now let us look at the tricks of multiplying two-digit numbers with 11

Example 2:

23 × 11 = ?

Step 1 (Copy):

Copy the first digit of the number from 23; **2** (it becomes the first digit at the hundreds' place in the answer)

Step 2 (Add):

Next, add the two numbers 2 + 3 = **5** (it becomes the second digit at the tens' place in the answer)

Being a Mathematician

Step 3 (Copy):
Then, copy the last digit of the number, which is **3** (it becomes the third digit at the ones' place in the answer)
In other words,

23 × 11 = 2 (2 + 3) 3
            ↓   ↓   ↓
253   Copy Add Copy

Tickle the Thoughts:

1. Ask the children to try using the techniques mentioned for other multiplication tables and check their answers. Do they work?
2. Encourage them to write the answers of a multiplication table of their choice and check if the table follows a pattern.

Goals Achieved
- Increased ability to understand multiplication tricks
- Better ability to break down difficult information into easier and smaller bits of information
- Promotes eye hand co-ordination

Tick-tack Tips

1. Once they have mastered the tricks, ask them to tell you the time table without using their fingers. They will be able to tell you the table by mentally visualizing the curling and stretching of the fingers. Give them time to be accurate in their answers first and then speed up, if required.
2. Multiplication is faster by the use of the above-mentioned methods than when the traditional method is followed.

Activity–15

Fast-track Car Race!

RESOURCES REQUIRED

- Photograph of each player (3 players)
- Glue
- Black tape
- Floor space
- Toy cars
- Paper
- A pen
- A measuring tape

Getting Ready:

Keep the required resources ready.

Math Language:

1. The information given in the table is called 'Data'.
2. The table given is called a 'picture graph'.
3. A picture used to represent an item or an object is called a 'symbol'. Representing information with the help of pictures is called the 'pictorial representation of data'.

Method to Make the Table:

1. Ask the children to draw four columns and four rows on the sheet.

86 Being a Mathematician

2. Ask them to use the measuring tape to measure the distance travelled by the car from the start line to the place where the car stopped on the track.
3. In the second, third and the fourth boxes in the top row, write the names of the car owners—Sid, Gugzee and Jugnu, respectively.
4. In the first column, write the ranking of the cars depending upon the maximum distance travelled by each car.
5. Each child gets to draw his or her car in front of the ranking written in the first column.

Distance travelled by the car (Starting from 0)	Sid	Gugzee	Jugnu
1			
2			
3			

Example 1:

How to Play:

1. Ask each player to stick the black tape on the floor to make racing tracks of equal lengths for their cars. Ask them to mark their tracks as 1, 2 and 3.
2. Then, ask them to mark a starting line, from where they will give their cars a push.
3. Now, hand over the paper to the players and help them draw the table given on the previous page.
4. Ask the players to record the distance travelled by their cars.
5. Allow the children to push their cars from the start line.
6. Refer to the table given below to record the distance travelled.

Activity—15 87

Distance travelled by the car (Starting from 0)	Sid	Gugzee	Jugnu
1		🚗	
2	🚙		
3			🚗

Tickle the Thoughts:

1. Ask the children to count the number of cars.
2. Ask them whose car travelled the maximum distance.
3. Ask them who won or lost the race.

> **Goals Achieved**
> - Improved math language
> - Improved problem-solving skills
> - Increased reasoning abilities
> - Better understanding of visual skills—pictorial representation of data
> - Enhanced and advanced understanding about the relationships among quantities when they sketch diagrams or draw tables

Tick-tack Tip

In the given example, children are asked to play a game, relate and represent the data on the given table. In the next pictograph, children will be asked to relate the symbols, and then in the next level of pictorial representation of data, children will be asked to use a key to represent a larger numerical data. All the three pictographs focus on developing different types of reasoning skills based on visual representations of data. The mentioned hierarchy of steps needs to be followed for the child to understand pictographs.

Activity—16

Pictograph!

RESOURCES REQUIRED
- Printouts of pictographs
- Pens

Getting Ready:

Keep the required resources ready.

Note: Pictographs are the visual representation of data.

Method:

1. When the children have to work on a large amount of numerical data, they need to use a 'symbol' to represent more than one object or item of the data.
2. We need to provide a clue to the player to represent the large data. This 'clue' is called the 'key'.
3. Key is written at the bottom of the table.
4. The key indicates the quantity represented by each picture or symbol.

Question 1:

Children are trained for table tennis, football and cricket. Four children are playing table tennis, nine are playing football, and ten are playing cricket. Represent the data using symbols:

Being a Mathematician

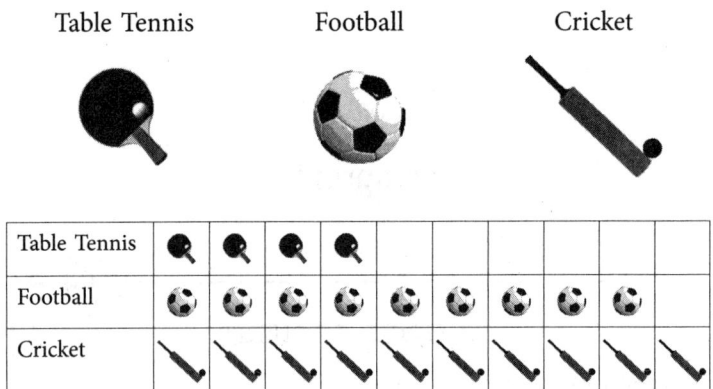

Table Tennis	🏓	🏓	🏓	🏓						
Football	⚽	⚽	⚽	⚽	⚽	⚽	⚽	⚽	⚽	
Cricket	🏏	🏏	🏏	🏏	🏏	🏏	🏏	🏏	🏏	🏏

Question 2:

Sid's friends like yoga, karate, music and dance. The pictorial graph of the same is given. Read it and answer the questions (in Tickle the Thoughts section).

Yoga	👤	👤	👤	👤			
Karate	👤	👤	👤	👤	👤		
Music	👤	👤	👤	👤	👤		
Dance	👤	👤	👤	👤	👤	👤	👤
Key 👤 = 5 students							

Tickle the Thoughts:

1. Ask the children what does 👤 represent.
2. Ask them in which activity do the least number of Sid's

Activity—16

friends take part.
3. Ask the children which activity do Sid's friends enjoy the most.
4. If each friend takes part in only one activity, ask the children how many friends will Sid have only in the first activity.
5. Ask them how many friends enjoy yoga.

Goals Achieved
- Increased math language
- Improved problem-solving skills
- Increased reasoning abilities
- Better understanding of visual skills—pictorial representation of data
- Enhanced and advanced understanding about the relationships among quantities when they sketch diagrams or draw tables

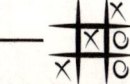

Tick-tack Tip
You can vary the value of the key as per the multiplication table you want the children to revise.

51	52	53	54	55	56	57	58	59	60
41	42	43	44	45	46	47	48	49	50
31	32							39	40
21	22		Verbal					29	30
11	12		Learning Style					19	20
1	2							9	10

Activity—17

Rapid-fire Multiplication!

> ### RESOURCES REQUIRED
> - Two papers
> - A pen
> - A stopwatch

Getting Ready:

1. Keep a stopwatch ready.
2. Keep about 15 multiplicands and multiplier flashcards ready.

How to Play:

1. Ask Sid, Guppy, Gugzee and Jugnu to sit in a circle in front of you in a way that each one of them can look at you, without their line of vision getting obstructed by another child.
2. Now ask Sid to show the multiplication flashcards to Guppy to give the answer to the sum on it. As soon as Guppy gives the answer, ask Sid to show the next flashcard to Guppy.
3. Ask Gugzee to mark the correct answers with a ☺ on a separate sheet. (Refer to the 'assessment sheet' to be given Gugzee on the following page). You may also create a fresh sheet as per your requirements.
4. Set timers and the child who gives the most number of accurate answers in the least amount of time becomes the winner.

96 Being a Mathematician

Name of the Child (Guppy)	Flash card (Sid shows the flash cards to Guppy)	Answer (Gugzee checks the answers given by Guppy)	☺ (For every correct answer, Gugzee puts a happy smiley in front of the correct answer)
	1 × 8	8	☺
	5 × 2	10	☺
	3 × 5	15	☺
	4 × 6	20	
	6 × 4	24	☺
	9 × 0	0	☺
			☺ = 5

Tip: Make sure that the *focus remains on accuracy* and *then* build on speed and not vice versa.

5. Give each child their turn to:
   - Ask questions
   - Give answers
   - Assess the results
   - Remember to count the 'happy smileys' to keep the child encouraged.

Tickle the Thoughts:

1. Ask the first child: what were you thinking when you were asking questions to Guppy?
2. Ask the second child: Why is giving a sad smiley not allowed? (Involve feelings)
3. Ask the third child: What was the second question asked by [the first child] to [the second child]?

Goals Achieved

- Enhanced mental calculations
- Builds on accuracy
- Enhanced recall speed
- Promoted listening skills
- Encourages to ask relevant questions
- Increased ability for giving relevant answers
- Assessing the answers given by the child and giving a corresponding results
- Increased understanding about data handling

Tick-tack Tips

- If the children are more in number, form separate teams—one to ask questions and the other to give answers.
- Ask the teams to come up with their own secret questions to ask the opponent team.
- To further enhance the mental calculations, set the stopwatch at 1 minute. Gradually reduce the time for retrieval of information. It means that increase the number of flash cards shown to the child per minute.

Activity—18

Division with Building Blocks!

RESOURCES REQUIRED

- Building blocks
- 2 feet long shoelace/ribbon

Getting Ready:

Keep the old building blocks and an old shoelace for making a learning tool (toy) with your child.

Method:

1. Ask the children to use a large rectangular piece of building blocks to form the base as shown in picture.
2. Ask the children to build equidistant 'buildings' of the same height. And number them 0–10.

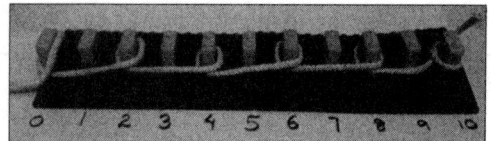

How to Play:

Next, explain the concept of division to the children. Repeated subtraction of the same number is called division. Division means sharing or dividing the total into equal parts.

Activity–18

Example 1:

To divide 10 by 2, or 10 ÷ 2, encourage the children to take the shoelace and wrap it around the buildings. Ask them to tie the shoelace around building number 10 and move backwards, two numbers at a time.

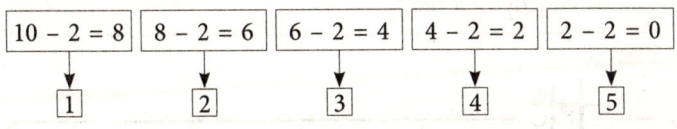

So, 10 ÷ 2 = 5

Tickle the Thoughts:

Now, ask the children if they can see any relation between the answer '5' and the number of jumps of the shoelace to get the answer.

Example 2:

Meet Sid, Guppy, Gugzee and Jugnu. They are best friends and want to play badminton together. They want to make teams. Divide them into 2 equal groups.

To divide 4 by 2, or 4 ÷ 2 = ?

So, 4 ÷ 2 = 2

Goals Achieved
- Better understanding of the concept of division
- Enhanced fine motor skills
- Promotes the concept of recycling the toys to use them as educational aids

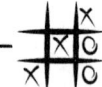

Tick-tack Tips

1. Introduce the children to the three important terms of division. Let us use the first example, 10 ÷ 2 = 5 to understand the following terms:
   - Dividend—The number which is to be divided is called the dividend—number 10
   - Divisor—The number which divides is called the divisor—number 2
   - Quotient—The number obtained by dividing the dividend and the divisor—number 5
2. Use the second example to further enhance the division skills of your child by introducing the names of your child's friends and help them practise division in real life. It gives the child the confidence to tackle division problems.

Activity–19

Trip to the Bank!

RESOURCES REQUIRED

- Coins
- Rupee notes—old and new
- Piggy bank
- Trip to the bank

Getting Ready:

1. Keep the coins and rupee notes ready.
2. Help children familiarize with the currency. In this example, let's use the Indian currency (the Rupee).

Note: By this age, children are aware that money can enable them to buy things. However, we need to make the children aware of what the 'value' of money is, and how we can use it in our day-to-day lives. Here, let's go about this activity in a slightly different manner. I would like to emphasize on the use of money in real life and not just using money to solve sums in notebooks. So, let us begin by explaining the very basics of money to the child before we take a trip to the bank.

Hand out a note to the child and ask him or her to tell you what they observe. After they have told you everything, introduce the unique features of the Indian currency to the child. The national currency notes of India reflect the nation's rich and diverse cultural heritage, its struggle for freedom and its commendable achievements. The currency has numerals in the Devanagari script and has a logo of Swachh Bharat. The new notes also have design elements in myriad and intricate forms and shapes.

Show them the unique security features in the current series of bank notes such as security thread, watermark, latent image of denomination numeral, denomination numeral in colour-shifting ink, number panels, see-through register, electrotype, bleed lines, etc.

1. In India, the unit of money is Rupee.
2. 1 Rupee = 100 Paise.
3. 'Re' or '₹' is the short form of Rupee.
4. 'Rs' or '₹' is the short form of Rupees.
5. We write rupees and paise separated by a dot, which is also called the decimal. For example, ₹15.50 = Fifteen rupees and fifty paise.
6. We convert rupees to paise by multiplying rupees by 100, since
   100p = Re 1
   Convert ₹23.50 to paise
   23.50 × 100 = 2350 paise
   We remove the decimal, or the dot, between rupees and paise to convert rupees to paise. We shift the decimal two places towards the right.
7. To convert paise to rupees, we divide by 100. For example, let's convert 10050 paise to rupees.
   10050 ÷ 100 = ₹100.50

When we divide a number by 100, we place the decimal point before the last two digits; i.e., we move the decimal towards the left.

Activity-19   103

Once children are familiar with the latest currency notes in use, ask them to take a piggy bank and start collecting coins for a week before you take them to the bank. Encourage them to count their savings.

- Children might not give you the money from their piggy bank for depositing it into 'your' account! Check with your bank if you can open a joint account with your child.
- Prepare for some extra pampering!

Share information such as:

1. Why do we need banks?
2. Where does the money come from into the bank? Who is a teller?
3. Where should you ask for help in a bank?
4. What is a bank account?
5. What is a chequebook, passbook, e-statement? Show the children where the bank account number is written on a chequebook.
6. What is a deposit slip? Show them how money can be deposited in a bank.
7. What are ATM cards, Debit and Credit cards? What is the difference between the three types of cards?
8. What is an ATM machine? How can they operate an ATM? What information do they require to operate the account?
9. How does the money get transferred into a different account? How do you receive a notification from the bank on your mobile phone?

Tickle the Thoughts:

1. Ask the children if you give them ₹100, what they would like to do with it.

2. Ask them how much money they will require to buy something.
3. How much money would they like to save out of the money they receive?

Goals Achieved
- Better understanding of the concept of money
- Increased ability to use money
- Enhanced finance management skills

Tick-tack Tips
1. Money is a very vast topic and many concepts can be taught. However, what goes amiss is the real use of money and its circulation in the market.
2. There are changes in the notes and coins that are in use nowadays. Update the children with the latest changes and share information about the old currency that was in use.
3. Introduce and encourage children to collect different currencies.
4. Whatever the amount you give the child, ensure that you monitor it. Ask them for a written record of their expenses and tell them to be accountable for their spending.
5. If they spend more than the budget, do not compensate it for any reason. Be persistent with your rules and you will teach them a lesson for life.

51	52	53	54	55	56	57	58	59	60
41	42	43	44	45	46	47	48	49	50
31	32							39	40
21	22			Social				29	30
11	12			Learning Style				19	20
1	2							9	10

Activity—20

Odds and Evens!

RESOURCES REQUIRED

- 3 A4-sized sheets
- A hole punch
- 1 chalk
- Floor space
- A pair of child-safe scissors
- 2 baskets

Interesting Facts about Odd and Even Numbers:

Even Numbers:

1. Check the last digit of a number to know if it is even. If the ones place has 0, 2, 4, 6 or 8, it is an even number.
2. All numbers divisible by two are even numbers.

Odd Numbers:

1. Check the last digit of a number to know if it is odd. If the ones place has 1, 3, 5, 7 or 9, it is an odd number.
2. All numbers not divisible by two are odd numbers.

Some More Interesting Facts:

1. Even number + even number = Even number

108 Being a Mathematician

2. Even number + odd number = Odd number
3. Odd number + odd number = Odd number
4. The sum of two odd numbers is never a prime number.
5. The sum of two even numbers is never a prime number.
6. A composite number may be even or odd.
7. The number 2 is the only prime number that is even.

Getting Ready:

Find an open space for the children to draw using chalks.

How to Play:

1. Ask the children to fold and cut the sheets into eight chits of equal sizes using child-safe scissors.
2. Ask them to punch holes into each chit or flash card with the hole punch.
3. Ask them to draw a start and a finish line on either sides of the floor.
4. Urge them to draw different shapes on the floor with chalks between the start and finish line.

Let us play:

1. Divide the children into two teams—Team 1 and Team 2. Line them up in front of the start line.
2. Hand over a basketful of flash cards that have holes punched into them.
3. On the count of three, ask them to run with their basket of flash-cards. Urge them to count the holes in the flash cards as they run. If the number of holes in a flash card is odd, they must be placed into the shape drawn on the floor with an odd number of sides. For example, if the number of holes in the flash card is 11, the child must place the flash card in

Activity-20

a shape that has 3, 5, 7 or 9 sides; for instance, a triangle. If the number of holes in the flash cards is even, say 4, the child must place the card in a shape that has an even number of sides, such as a square, rectangle, hexagon, octagon, etc.

4. They must place all the flash cards into the respective shapes before they race to the finish line.
5. The child who crosses the finish line with the maximum number of flash cards placed accurately inside the shapes is the winner.

Tickle the Thoughts:

1. Ask the children how many sides the shape nonagon has. Ask them if they can draw a nonagon on the floor?
2. Ask the children in each team to count the number of members. Tell the team with the odd number of players to stand or jump.

> **Goals Achieved**
> - Exercised motor skills—fine and gross motor
> - Enhanced speed of counting the dots
> - Better concept of shapes
> - Increased reasoning abilities

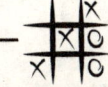

Tick-tack Tip
The game can be played with two opponents or all the children playing at the same time. In the latter case, you will require more number of baskets. You may also hand over the flash cards in their hands before the race.

Activity–21

Expanded Form!

RESOURCES REQUIRED

- 10 paper cups
- A pen
- Rubber band/elastic band

Getting Ready:

Keep the resources from the previous game ready.

Provocation:

1. Ask the children what the word 'expand' means.
2. Give them a rubber or an elastic band and a few minutes to play with it.
3. Ask them to tell you five uses of a rubber band.
4. Stretch and expand the rubber band to show them what the word 'expand' means.

Method:

1. Ask the children to take one paper cup at a time and write numbers from 0 to 9 along the brim of the cup. At the bottom of this cup, tell them to write 'ONES PLACE'.
2. Similarly, ask them to write the numbers for tens, hundreds thousands and so forth, and their corresponding names tens,

Activity—21 111

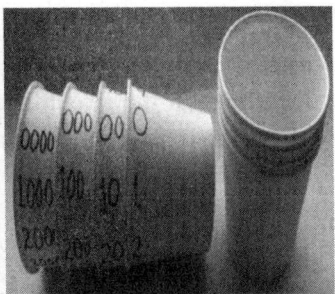

hundreds and thousands at the bottom of the cups.
3. Ask them to place a plus sign at the end of each number.

How to Play:

1. Give a number to a child such as 74,203.
2. Ask them to rotate the cups to align the numbers correctly to form 74,203.
3. Tell them to align all the plus signs on the cups such that they are visible.

Being a Mathematician

Tickle the Thoughts:

1. Ask them if they can form the same number on an abacus.
2. Ask them if they would like to expand bigger numbers.
3. Let them think of smaller and bigger numbers by themselves. Tell them to make a note of all formations by adding the values.
4. Ask them if they would like to explain to their friends the concept of 'expanded form'.

Goals Achieved
- Better understanding of the concept of expanded form
- Increased mentoring abilities
- Improved presentation skills

Tick-tack Tip

Once they have mastered the skill, ask them to demonstrate it to their friends at school or home. Let them rebuild the project all over again. It will help them understand the concept better with different perspectives.

Activity—22

Paper Dress!

> RESOURCES REQUIRED
> - Newspapers
> - A measuring tape
> - Sticking tape or a stapler

Getting Ready:

Keep the required resources ready.

Units for Measuring Length:

1. Kilometre (km): Used to measure very long distances such as the distance between Delhi and Mumbai.
2. Metre (m): Used to measure smaller distances or lengths such as the length of a track. It is the standard unit used to measure any length.
3. Foot (ft): Usually used to measure height of a person and is denoted by a single apostrophe (').
4. Inch (in): Often used to measure items such as a television and is denoted by double prime ("). For example, 2 feet 4 inches can be denoted as 2'4".
5. Centimetres (cm): Used to measure even smaller lengths such as the length of a pen.
6. To measure different lengths, we use measuring tools such

as a ruler and a tape.
7. Before these standardized measures were invented, people estimated length with the span of their hand, the lengths of their arm, their stride, etc., which were not precise.

Interesting Facts on Measurement:

1. 100 centimetres (cm) = 1 metre (m)
2. 1000 metres = 1 kilometre (km)
3. To convert metres into centimetres, multiply the number of metres by 100.
4. To convert kilometres to metres, multiply the number of kilometres by 1000.

How to Make a Measuring Tape:

1. Ask the children to draw lines 1" apart, along the length of the chart paper.
2. Ask them to cut out a horizontal strip using the child-safe scissors.
3. Now, ask them to mark centimetres on the opposite side of the 'inch' markings. Every marking should be 1 cm apart.
4. The inch tape is now ready for use.

How to Use:

Ask a child to stand still. Urge another child to measure his or her height, length of legs and arms, and write down the recordings on a piece of paper.

Method:

1. Ask the children to spread the double sheet of a newspaper on the table.
2. Ask them to measure the girth of the friend's waist to make a belt.

3. Instruct them to cut the newspaper as per the measurement and fold it into half; fold this half into another half to make a strip. The belt of the skirt is ready.
4. Ask the children to measure the length of the skirt—from the waist till the knee. Instruct them to follow the above-mentioned steps to make about 15 to 20 strips, which will hang from the belt.
5. Ask them to glue the belts to that made for the waist as shown in the picture.
6. Staple the strips with the belt to secure them. Try not stapling your friend along with it.
7. Then, ask them to carefully hold the skirt around the friend's waist and check if it fits her. Bring the two ends together and staple them. Ask her how the skirt fits.

Tickle the Thoughts:

1. Ask the children what helped them make the skirt well and how.
2. Ask them if they need measurements that are more precise and ways to get them.
3. Ask them how they can make a shirt or a top to match the skirt with.

Goals Achieved
- Better understanding about the concept and facts of measurement
- Exercised fine motor skills
- Enhanced creative thinking

Tick-tack Tip

If the belts of the skirt spread and leave gaps, make a few more belts and stick a newspaper from behind the belts.

Activity–23

Multiplication Tunnel!

> ### RESOURCES REQUIRED
> - 1 medium-sized ball per team
> - Paper chits
> - 1 basket

Getting Ready:

1. Keep a soft, medium-sized ball ready.
2. Ask the children to write the multiplication tables between 1 to10 on each of the chits.

How to Play:

1. Divide the players into two teams (Team A and B) and ask them to form a queue. Urge them to spread their legs to form a straight tunnel, with the gap between their two legs.
2. Now, call the first player of both the teams and ask each of them to pick up a chit from the basket. The respective team must answer the multiplication problem mentioned in the chit. For example, the first player from the Team A chooses a chit that reads 5 times 3. The player shouts out the answer to the question.
3. Then, you hand over a ball to the first player of each team and ask him or her to roll it through their respective tunnels.

Ask the other players of the team to not move or touch the ball with their feet when it rolls through the tunnel.
4. Ask the last player of the team to crouch and catch the ball.
5. The last player then runs to the front, picks a chit, shouts out the answer and runs to the front of the tunnel to roll the ball through the tunnel. (Now the second last player becomes the last player to catch the ball).
6. Every player in a team must get a chance to throw the ball through the tunnel. The fastest team wins.

Tickle the Thoughts:

Give the children multiplication word problems to solve. For example:

- If one book costs ₹5, how much will 10 books cost? (Answer = ₹50)
- If one chocolate costs ₹20, how much will 5 chocolates cost? (Answer = ₹100)

Goals Achieved
- Better understanding of multiplication properties
- Enhanced mental math
- Increased recall speed
- Encourages team work
- Promotes the ability to take turns
- Exercised gross motor skills

Tick-tack Tip

Introduce skip counting. Ask children to solve problems such as skip count 2s (Answer: 2, 4, 6, 8, 10, 12, and so on). The parent/teacher can chose the number to skip count depending on what you plan to revise with children.

Activity–24

Dice and Coins!

```
RESOURCES REQUIRED
► Lots of coins
► A dice
► An empty bowl
```

Getting Ready:

Ask the children to make a circle. Place a bowlful of coins of different denominations at the centre of the circle.

How to Play:

Ask the players to take turns to roll the dice and take as many coins as is shown on the dice.

For example: If the child rolls a 6, the child takes ₹6 coins from the bowl. It is up to them to take three ₹2 coins or take one ₹5 and one ₹1 coin, and so on. The total amount of coins collected is added up when all the coins in the bowl are used up. The child with the maximum amount of coins wins the game.

Tickle the Thoughts:

1. Ask the children what if they played the game with two dice. What will be the biggest number rolled?

2. Ask them if they can name the different denominations of ₹100.

> ## Goals Achieved
> - Better understanding of addition and subtraction facts
> - Enhanced understanding of the concept of money
> - Promotes turns-taking ability
> - Encourages to break-down a bigger number into its smaller denominations

Tick-tack Tip
As the children master the game, use different currencies with bigger denominations.

Activity—25

Race without the Crown!
(4-digit Multiplication without Carrying-over)

RESOURCES REQUIRED
- 15 papers
- A Pen
- Thread/Ribbon–1 roll
- 1 hole punch

Getting Ready:

1. Divide the children into three teams—A, B and C.
2. Team A and Team C should have 4 and 10 players, respectively, and Team B should have 1 player.
3. Ask all the players to take a paper each and punch a hole on the side of the paper. Pass a thread through the holes. Urge them to make the loop of their number cards big enough to easily pass their heads through it.
4. Next, ask Team A to write one multiplicand number from '1234' on their respective number cards. Team B should write 2 on his or her number card. Team C players should write one number from 0 to 9 on their respective number cards. Then, ask them to wear their number cards around their neck.
5. Teams A and C should stand on the opposite sides facing

Activity—25   **123**

each other and the player of Team C should stand at the centre of the ground.

Only the players with the number cards 2468 will get the chance to run to the finish line. (In the next multiplication chase, you can have sums that will offer opportunity for the other players to run).

6. Draw a finish line on the ground. It is where the multiplicands and their products will hold hands and run to finish the game.
7. Multiply each place in turn, beginning from the ones' place, which is number 4, then tens, hundreds and lastly thousands.

Clickety-click, How to Trick:

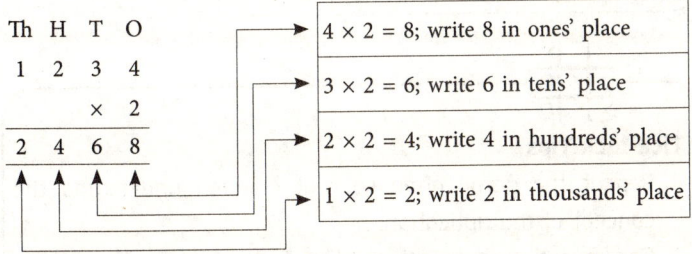

How to Play:

1. Now, at the count of three, the multiplicand at the ones' place and its product run towards the finish line. The denner then chases to catch them before the multiplicand number '4' reaches its product number 8.
2. The multiplicand and the product dodge the multiplier to hold hands and race together towards the finish line.
3. Next, the chase begins for the number at the tens' place, which is 3 and so forth.

Being a Mathematician

Tickle the Thoughts:

1. Ask the children what will happen if the product has a number bigger than 9, say 10.
2. Ask the product team: Can the digits 1 and 0 team up to cross the ground without the denner catching them? What will happen to number 1? Introduce 'Multiplication with the Crown', the carry-over multiplication!

Goals Achieved
- Better understanding of multiplication facts
- Promotes team spirit
- Exercises gross and fine motor skills

Tick-tack Tips
1. Repeat the game often so that children understand the concept of multiplication.
2. Continue the game till children begin to take the risk to think and come up with answers/solutions to 'Tickle the Thoughts'. They may give estimates as answers, but welcome all the kinds of thought processes. Remember to encourage 'mathematical thinking' at every opportunity.

Activity—26

Race with the Crown!
(4-digit Multiplication with Carry-over)

RESOURCES REQUIRED

- A chart paper
- Glue
- A packet of glitter
- A pair of child-safe scissors
- A stapler with pins

For the Crown
- 15 sheets of paper
- A pen
- Thread/ribbon—1 roll
- 1 hole punch

Making the Crown

Getting Ready:

1. Take the chart paper and cut 15-cm-wide and 50-cm-long strips.
2. Now, ask the children to fold along the width of the chart paper into half and press it to form a crease. Then, ask the children to open the chart paper and, using the child-safe scissors, cut one half of the crease to form small mountains around the length or the girth of the crown.

Being a Mathematician

3. Next, ask them to spread the glue on one side of the crown and sprinkle glitters on it. Allow it to dry.
4. Help the players to wear the crowns on their heads.
5. Carefully staple it to secure its ends. The carry-over crowns are ready.

How to Play:

1. Give the papers, pens and threads to all the players to write the assigned numbers.
2. Now, ask the players to make four teams—A, B, C and D.
3. Team A should have 4 players. Assign a number to each of them, as they will be the multiplicands 1698.
4. Team B should have 10 players. Ask them to choose a number from 0 to 9 and write them down on their papers, as they will represent the products.
5. Team C can have a minimum of 3 players, as they will represent the carry-over numbers. Ask them to wear their crowns.
6. Team D will be the denner, the multiplier number 2, who stands a the centre of the ground.
7. Ask all the children to punch holes on the sides of the paper and pass a thread through it. Urge them to wear it around their neck like an identity card.
8. Draw lines on the three sides of the ground, where Teams A, B and C will stand.
9. Draw a finish line on the fourth side of the ground; the multiplicand, the product along with the crown, will hold hands and race towards this line.

Activity—26   127

Clickety-click, How to Trick:

1. STEP 1:

Th	H	T	O
1	6	9	8
		×	2

   > STEP 1
   > Ask the children to arrange the numbers neatly on a piece of paper.

2. STEP 2:

   Th H T O

   ```
   1  6  9  8
         × 2
   ─────────
             6
   ```

   > STEP 2:
   > 8 × 2 = 16 Ones
   > = 1 Tens + 6 Ones.
   > Write 6 at ones place and carry 1 ten

3. STEP 3:

   Th H T O

   ```
   1  6  9  8
         × 2
   ─────────
          9  6
   ```

   > STEP 3:
   > 9 × 2 = 18 Tens
   > = 18 Tens + 1 Tens = 19 Tens.
   > 1 Hundred + 9 Tens.
   > Write 9 tens and carry 1 hundred.

4. STEP 4:

   Th H T O

   ```
   1  6  9  8
         × 2
   ─────────
       3  9  6
   ```

   > STEP 4:
   > 6 × 2 = 12 Hundreds.
   > 12 Hundreds + 1 Hundred
   > = 1 Thousand + 3 Hundreds.
   > Write 3 hundreds and carry 1 thousand.

5. STEP 5:

Th	H	T	O
♛	♛	♛	
1	6	9	8
		×	2
3	3	9	6

STEP 5:
1 × 2 = 2 Thousands.
2 Thousands + 1 Thousand
= 3 Thousand
Write 3 thousands. ♛

So, the product is **3396**

How to Play:

1. Ask number 1 from Team C to wear the crown (signifying the carry-over) and couple with number 6 from Team A. Numbers 1 and 6 should hold hands, dodge the denner (Team D) and reach the finish line with number 8 from Team B.
2. Once the multiplicand, the product, along with the crown, have successfully reached the finish line, the next multiplicand, 9, is positioned at 'tens' place and the chase begins again.
3. If the denner catches the multiplicand, the product or the crown, the game is over. The denner now takes a position in Team B, and the player who was caught during the chase becomes the denner.

Tickle the Thoughts:

1. Ask the entire group of children: Who would like to be the multiplier?
2. If Sid chooses a bigger number, such as 5, ask him how many crowns (carry-over players) will be needed to run to the finish line? Increase the number of crown players accordingly.

Activity—26

🎯 Goals Achieved
- Better understanding of concept of carry-over in multiplication
- Promotes team work
- Exercises gross and fine motor skills

Tick-tack Tips
1. The products can wear capes; the multiplicands and the denner can choose to make swords made of corrugated sheet, wrapped with silver foil!
2. Ask the multiplier to help all the players to revise the complete table to the entire group of children. Supposing Sid chooses to be the denner and to be the multiplier of 5. Then, Sid helps the other players to revise the table of 5.

Activity—27

Garage Sales!

RESOURCES REQUIRED

- Time
- Paper and pencil
- Chalk boards and chalks
- Cardboard
- Markers
- An ad in the local newspaper/social media
- Items for sale
- Price tags

Getting Ready:

1. A garage sale is a big project and children will require guidance and support to make it a success.
2. Keep plenty of time in hand to unearth the junk in the house for the children to sell and earn some money.
3. Involving neighbour's children in organizing the sale will help you delegate work and share the responsibility.
4. Encourage the children to tidy up the house and gather all items that they do not need or use any more, such as old toys, games, old CDs, storybooks, schoolbooks, magazines, clothes, linen, furniture, bean bags, etc.

Activity-27   131

Pricing the Items for Garage Sale:

1. Once the children have collected the items to be sold in the garage sale, help them to sort, order, compare and classify them.
2. Next, ask them to guess the original price at which you had purchased the item. For example, a bat that you had brought for them during their summer vacations was for ₹500. (Introduce the concept of retail price to them.) Help them see the MRP label on various items that you have recently purchased for personal use.
3. Make word problems relevant to the sale. Help them understand the profit they will make by selling the items.
4. Allow the children to come up with their estimations for each item.
5. Encourage them to fold and pack the items neatly.
6. Now, hand over the price tags to them.
7. Then, ask them how much they would like to sell the item (for instance, the bat) for.
8. Encourage them to come up with a reasonable 'selling price'.
9. Encourage them to write and stick the decided price for each item at an easily visible place for the customers to read.
10. Once all the items have been smartly packed, priced and labelled, keep them aside.

Advertising the Sale:

1. Next, ask them how the people will know about the 'Garage Sale'.
2. Help them to come up with a script for an ad to be placed at various places in the vicinity. (Check if you need permission for placing the ad in public places and provide the required support).

To write the ad, they will have to know the time, date and venue for the sale! Ask them to zero down the details so that they can give clear information to the customers.

3. They can write the ad on a chalkboard and place it in front of the garage. This can be done three days before the sale. It will give the customers time to plan for the sale.
4. Help the children to draw and write the details of the sale on chart papers, including directions to the venue.

Tickle the Thoughts:

1. Ask them what they would like to do with the money that they collect.
2. Ask the children if they would like to donate to the lesser privileged.
3. Ask them what does 'reduce and recycle' means.

Goals Achieved
- Improved math language
- Increased literacy skills
- Improved ability to estimate
- Improved ability to plan
- Better understanding of the concept of pricing
- Better understanding of addition and subtraction of money
- Enhanced organization skills

Activity–27

Tick-tack Tip

Introduce the concept of 'empathy' by helping the lesser privileged with the money they collect. Encourage the children to appreciate greater things in life. A simple pat on the shoulder to appreciate their hard work should make them feel rewarded instead of getting them material things.

51	52	53	54	55	56	57	58	59	60
41	42	43	44	45	46	47	48	49	50
31	32							39	40
21	22		Solitary					29	30
11	12		Learning Style					19	20
1	2							9	10

Activity–28

Place Value Kit!

> ### RESOURCES REQUIRED
> - 10 paper cups
> - A pen

Getting Ready:

Get plain paper cups, which have no texts or prints on them.

Place and Face Values:

1. Explain to the children that just as you have a face and place to live, the digits in a number, too, have their face values and place values. Their place values depend on their positions in the ones, tens or hundreds place.
2. To know which number is greater between two, check the place value of each digit. Ask the children to first compare the hundreds place; then, compare the tens; and finally, compare the ones place. The number with the digits having greater place value is the bigger number.
3. In case the place values are the same, ask the children to check the face values of the digits in both numbers. The number with the larger face value will form the bigger number.
4. Similarly, if the face value of the hundreds and tens digits is the same; then ask the children to check the face value of

Being a Mathematician

the digit on the ones place. For example, if the numbers are 361, 362 and 363, then the order will be 363 > 362 > 361.

Place Value:

- Let us understand place value with an example:
- Check the place value of the number 7 in 2479.
- The place value of the number 7 in 2479 is 70, or 7 tens, as it is placed at the tens place.

Face Value:

- The Face Value is the number itself without considering its placement.
- Let us understand face value with the same example:
- The face value of 7 in 2479 is 7.

Place Value and Face Value of a 5-digit number:

For example, let us consider the number 24,679,

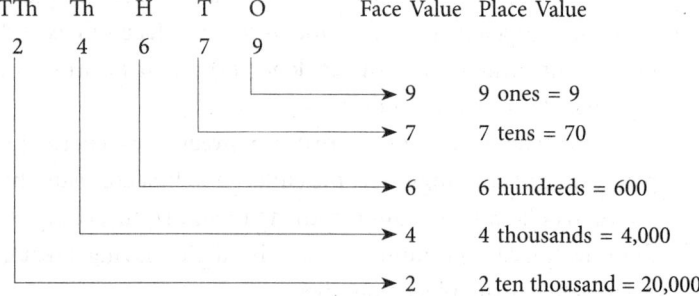

How to Make the Kit:

1. Ask the children to take one paper cup at a time and write numbers from 0 to 9 along the brim of the cup. At the bottom of this cup, urge them to write

'ONES PLACE'.

2. Similarly, ask them to write the numbers for tens, hundreds thousands and so forth, and their corresponding names tens, hundreds and thousands at the bottom of the cups.

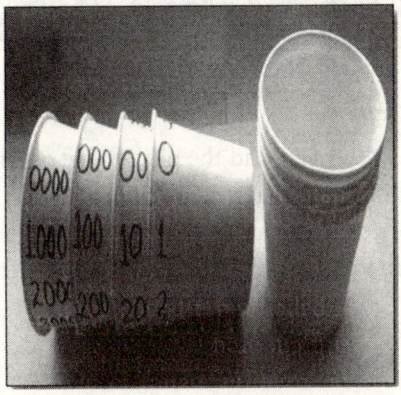

How to Play:

1. Give a number to a child, such as 3579, and ask him or her its place value. For example, what is the place value of 5 in this number?

2. Ask the child to rotate the cups to align them such that it forms the correct number.
3. Urge them to separate the cups and note the reading for 5. Ask them to check the bottom of the cup to know the place value.
4. This cup represents the hundreds place. Therefore, the place value of 5 is 5 hundreds = 500.

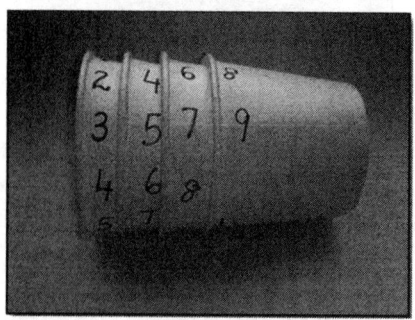

Tickle the Thought:

1. Ask them if they can find the place value of 6 in the number 4689, without using the cups?
2. Ask them what else can be used to create the same project. Allow them to come up with more ideas, and let them execute them.

> **Goals Achieved**
> - Better understanding of Face Value and Place Value
> - Increased mentoring abilities
> - Improved presentation skills

Activity-28

Tick-tack Tips
1. Ask the children to play with an abacus. It helps to revise concepts.
2. Once they have mastered the skill, ask them to demonstrate their skills in front of their friends at school or home. Let them rebuild the project.

Activity–29

Planning!

RESOURCES REQUIRED

- Time
- Paper and pencil

Getting Ready:

1. Keep plenty of time in hand to have an open-ended conversation with children.
2. Keep a piece of paper and a pencil ready for each child

Method:

1. Discuss a few daily jobs to do with the children.
2. Now write down a 'rewards list' on a piece of paper. Ask the children to draw or write a list of things that they would like to get as a reward. Encourage them to come up with healthy choices and rewards that will add to their hobbies, such as a football or a cricket bat, a special dessert that you can help them make, a visit to a botanical garden or even a library to pick up their favourite books!
3. Then, involve them in making a list of jobs/assignments on a piece of paper, and ask them to decide which job they would like to take up. Make them write their names against the job mentioned.

4. Ensure that everyone in the family encourages children to achieve their goals.
5. Every time the child does the job, ask him or her to pick the desired reward from the reward list. Ensure you save up extra money for the rewards.

Tickle the Thoughts:

1. Against each reward in the list, ask the children to write its cost. For example, if the child chooses to go to the botanical garden, ask the child to estimate the cost of logistics.
2. Increase the number of people going to the botanical garden with them. Ask the child to estimate the increase or decrease in the cost. Encourage them to do the calculations.
3. Make word problems for the children and encourage them to do mental calculations and come up with an estimate or an approximate answer.
4. Encourage them to take the initiative and plan a trip. Help them do all the planning. They might not be professionals yet, but it is never too early to sow the seeds of a future finance expert.

Goals Achieved
- Improved skills for estimation and rounding
- Improved addition and subtraction abilities
- Better understanding of the concept of multiplication and division
- Enhanced ability to plan
- Increased sense of responsibility

Tick-tack Tips

1. As the reward list gets exhausted, create a new one till the children internalize the sense of responsibility and master the art of planning.

2. During the entire process, remember to genuinely appreciate the progress the child has made without talking about the rewards in terms of 'money.' Appreciate their job in front of your family and friends. This will help them to internalize responsibility that comes with the job. Soon, they will shoulder the responsibility and the 'reward' will lose its brilliance. They would have already learnt how to do the planning. We will be in a 'win-win' situation with nothing to lose!

Activity–30

Shopping Calculations with Calculator

RESOURCES REQUIRED
- A paper
- A pencil
- A calculator
- A trip to a shopping mall

Getting Ready:
Keep a calculator with large number keys ready.

How to Play:
1. Ask the children to take a paper and a pencil each.
2. Share information about various keys on the calculator. Show them how to press the number keys and how to clear numbers on display.
3. Next, write a few numbers on the paper for them to copy. Once they have mastered the tricks; take them to a shopping mall and call out simple word problems for them to solve.

Tickle the Thoughts:
Ask them questions such as:

Q. 1. A blue t-shirt costs ₹200 and a red t-shirt costs ₹300. How much money do I need to spend to buy both the t-shirts for you?

Q. 2. One jean costs ₹500. How much will two jeans cost?

Give enough time to the child to use the calculator and give you the answer.

> ###  Goals Achieved
> - Better understanding of various mathematical concepts
> - Increased understanding about how gadgets can be used for purposeful learning
> - Exercised fine motor skills

Tick-tack Tip

As children begin to develop interest in using the calculator, share information with them about how a machine can give precise answers to complex calculations in negligible time.

Activity–31

Working Model of a Clock!

RESOURCES REQUIRED

- 1 corrugated sheet
- 1 craft paper
- 1 pair of child-safe scissors
- Felt Pens
- A glue gun
- Clock mechanism
- Battery

Getting Ready:

Keep the required resources ready.

Method:

1. Ask the children to cut out an 8 cm × 8 cm square from a corrugated sheet and the craft paper. Stick the craft paper on the corrugated sheet to make the face of the clock.
2. Ask them to cut out and paste squares measuring 2 cm × 2 cm from the remaining craft paper and write the clock numbers on them.
3. Ask them to cut 12 squares of 1 cm × 1 cm each and write down the multiples of 5. These will become the markings for minutes.

148 Being a Mathematician

	55	60	5		
X	11	12	1	X	
50	10			2	10
45	9			3	15
40	8			4	20
X	7	6	5	X	
	35	30	25		

4. Ask them to paste these along the perimeter of the face of the clock as shown in the picture.
5. Drill a hole at the centre of the clock.
6. Help them to use the glue gun to attach the clock's mechanism from behind the corrugated sheet and the hands of the clock to the centre of the dial. Secure it with screws.
7. Ask them to place the battery.
8. The clock is ready for use.

Tickle the Thoughts:

1. Ask the children what the clock does.
2. Ask them what the hourglass and the sundial do.
3. Ask them to explain the markings on the battery.
4. Tell them to measure the time taken for them to finish their favourite food.
5. Ask them what being early or late means and when do they hear these words in the morning.
6. Ask them if it is good to be early or late or on time for a birthday party and why.

Activity-31

🎯 Goals Achieved
- Better understanding of the concept of time
- Understanding of the mechanism of a clock
- Exercised fine motor skills

Tick-tack Tips
1. Discuss the important activities children do during the day. Ask them to draw illustrations of four important activities they do and stick them on the face of the clock. The illustrations can be pasted on the clock corresponding to the time at which they perform them.
2. Children may write roman numerals made with matchsticks for writing the clock's numbers.
3. Discuss with them why it is important to be on time.

51	52	53	54	55	56	57	58	59	60
41	42	43	44	45	46	47	48	49	50
31	32							39	40
21	22		Naturalistic					29	30
11	12		Learning Style					19	20
1	2							9	10

Activity–32

Sunny Sundials!

RESOURCES REQUIRED

- An 8"-wide paper plate
- A ruler
- Play dough
- Crayons
- A pencil

Getting Ready:

Keep the required resources ready.

How to Make:

1. Ask the children to mark the centre of the paper plate with the marker.
2. Ask them to write '12' anywhere on the circumference of the plate.
3. Now, place the ruler at 12 and align it with the centre of the plate. Ask the children to draw a straight line across the plate through the centre to meet the other side of the circumference.
4. Ask them to roll a small ball of play dough and place it at the centre of the plate.
5. Ask the children to fix the pencil vertically on the play dough,

making a right angle.
6. On a sunny day, ask the children to head outdoors at twelve 'o clock with newly created sundial. The sun will cast a shadow of the pencil on the plate.
7. Adjust the shadow of the pencil such that it falls exactly on the marking (12) on the plate.
8. As time passes by, the shadow of the pencil will move. Ask the children to record their observations after every 15 minutes.
9. Ensure that they do not move the sundial while marking their observations on it.

Tickle the Thoughts:

1. Ask them if the sundial shows the exact time.
2. Ask them how they will know the time on a rainy day.

Goals Achieved
- Better understanding of the concept of time
- Exercised fine motor skills
- Increased reasoning abilities

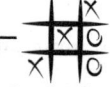

Tick-tack Tips

1. In ancient times, sundials were the instruments used for telling time. The surface of a sundial has markings for each hour of daylight. As the sun moves across the sky, the sundial casts a shadow on these markings. The position of the shadow shows what time it is.
2. To position a horizontal sundial correctly, you will need to find the exact directions of north or south. The pencil, set to

Activity-32

the correct latitude, has to point to the exact South if you are in the Southern hemisphere, and if you are in the northern hemisphere it has to point to the exact North.

3. The Jaipur Observatory in Rajasthan, which contains the Jantar Mantar instruments, is the largest and best preserved of the ancient big observatories.
4. The Samrat Yantra is the world's largest sundial.

Activity–33

Estimate the Distance!

RESOURCES REQUIRED

- A long car ride
- A watch
- A road map

Getting Ready:

This game can be played during long and tedious car rides. All you need is someone to time the game.

How to Play:

1. As you drive, have one of the children check the road map.
2. Ask another child to estimate the distance from your current location to the destination.
3. The driver checks and announces the kilometres from the current location on the speedometer and after reaching the destination.
4. The player with the closest estimation is the winner.

Tickle the Thoughts:

1. Ask the children why they need to measure distance in kilometres.
2. Ask them why they need to have 'standardized' measures.

3. Ask them what are milestones and where is 'zero mile'.
4. How else can we measure the distance?

Goals Achieved
- Better understanding of the concept of estimation
- Enhanced spatial sense
- Better understanding about the concept of time and distance

Tick-tack Tip

The British considered Nagpur to be the geographical centre of India. It was constructed during the British rule in India and used as the starting point to calculate, or measure, the distance between states/towns and Nagpur. After the Partition of India and Pakistan, the centre of the country shifted from Nagpur to a small village in Madhya Pradesh. The geographical centre point of modern India is located in Karaundi, Betul, Madhya Pradesh.

Activity—34

Probably Yes, Probably No!

RESOURCES REQUIRED

- Printouts of the pictures with animals
- 7 animal cut-outs
- 2 paper cups
- A marker/pen

Getting Ready:

You will require seven cutouts of animals for the diagram. In this example, let us add three snakes, two koalas, one alpaca and a fox.

Note: This activity is explained in two stages. First, where the children will understand the concept of probability, and in the second stage, they will understand it through a story and represent the probability on a table. Both the activities have separate 'Tickle the Thoughts'.

Definition:

Probability is the chance that an event might occur. Let us represent probability with the letter 'P'.

It means that $P \text{ (event)} = \dfrac{\text{Number of favourable outcomes}}{\text{Total number of possible outcomes}}$

This sounds very theoretical! So, let us understand it with a simpler definition:

$$P\,(\text{event}) = \frac{\text{How many things will make a person} ☺/☹}{\text{Total number of things}}$$

Probability can be explained to the children in many simple ways. Another simple method is by using the Probability Line.

As already explained, probability is the chance that an event will happen. Assume the probability of an event occurring is somewhere between impossible and certain on the Probability Line mentioned below.

Let us assume that the probability of an event to occur is **impossible** at 0 and that the probability of an event to take place is **certain** at 10.

Example 1:

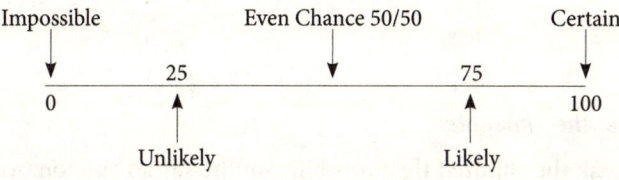

Example 2:

Probability with Fractions:

Let us assume that the probability of an event to occur is impossible at 0 and that the probability of an event to take place is certain at 1.

160 Being a Mathematician

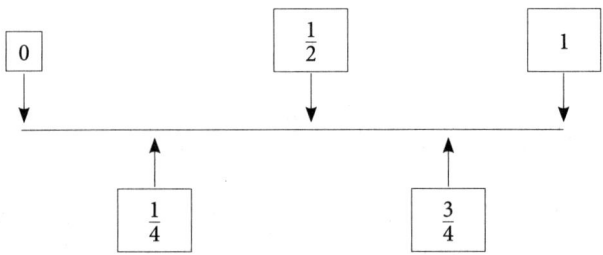

Example 3:

Probability with Percentages:
Let us assume that the probability of an event to occur if impossible at 0 per cent and that the probability of an event to take place is certain at 100 per cent.

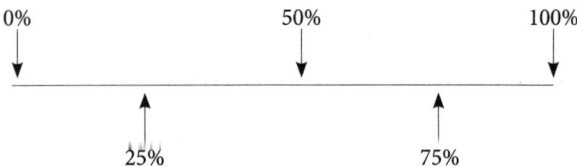

Tickle the Thoughts:

1. Ask the children the probability of the sun to rise tomorrow. (100%)
2. Ask them the probability of not being able to learn mathematics at school. (0%)
3. What is the probability of choosing a red jelly bean from a bag with one red jelly bean and three yellow jelly beans? (25%)
4. Ask them how else they can represent probability. (Use a glass jar, make equidistant markings with the help of a marker on it, and pour water into the jar to show probability using liquids).

Activity-34   161

Activity continues:

Area Model:

Let us understand probability with the help of interesting animals in the jungle:

1. Ask the children to take two cups and label them as 1 and 2.
2. Encourage them to abbreviate all the names of the animals, such as 'K' for Koala, 'A' for Alpaca, and so on.
3. Ask them to put any three animal cutouts in Cup 1 and any four in Cup 2.
4. Ask them to make a rectangle with a pen or marker. Now, tell them to place the three animal cutouts from Cup 1 on the vertical line of the rectangle in the given diagram (the vertical bark of the tree—the Y-axis). Ask them to place the animal cutouts from Cup 2 on the horizontal line of the rectangle (the horizontal bark of the tree—the X-axis).
5. Next, ask them to take the marker and draw four vertical lines and four horizontal lines as done in the figure 'Probability Area Model' on the previous page.

   You will get 12 small boxes in the Probability Area Model, which means that we can expect 12 probable outcomes. Keep it aside and offer the children to read the story 'Lost in the Jungle' mentioned below.

Lost in the Jungle

It was late in the evening when Guppy was playing football with his friends near the jungle. Sid kicked the ball hard and it flew into the jungle. Guppy decided to go looking for his football. As he searched for the ball, he was tempted to go further into the jungle.

Suddenly, Guppy looked around and realized that he was lost in the scary, dark jungle. The raspy bark of the foxes made him sweat profusely in the cold evening. He saw something move on the tree—slithery and long—and he asked himself, 'Is that a snake?' He goes closer to the tree to get a better glimpse. To his surprise, there was not just one snake, but there were two snakes on the tree. He turned pale with fear and screamed, 'Oh My God!' and started running frantically, hoping that his parents would come looking for him before it got pitch dark.

As he ran further away from the tree, he saw an animal, which resembled a horse, but it was an alpaca! He was tired but decided not to stop running. On reaching a huge rock, he stopped to catch a breath and climbed on to it. He sat on the rock, still scared, and put his head on his knees, closed his eyes and started to think about the probability of the different animals that could get to him. He thought to himself, 'What is the probability of reaching home safely if he rode an alpaca?'

NOTE: Introduce the below-mentioned graph to the children. Point out the animals on the (vertical) tree and point out the four animals on the (horizontal) tree log. Next, ask them to make the combinations or the outcomes by using one name of the animal on the tree and one name of the animal on the tree log. For example, koala (K) and fox (F) makes the first probability outcome at the lowest left corner, and so forth. Once the children have arrived at all the possible outcomes, introduce the equation once again:

$$P \text{ (event)} = \frac{\text{How many things will make a person ☺/☹}}{\text{Total number of things}}$$

Activity–34   163

$$P(\text{event}) = \frac{\text{The safest combination of koala and alpaca} \ \odot}{\text{Total number of animals}} = \frac{1}{12}$$

Help the children to find the safest combination of animals that Guppy could use to reach home $= \frac{1}{12}$

The story continues…

Just then, a beam of light flashed, penetrating the darkness of the jungle. He looked up and heard a familiar voice call-out his name. 'Guppy, Guppy, are you there?' It was his mother's voice. The moment Guppy heard her voice, he screamed, 'Yes, Mommy! I am over here!' He ran as fast as he could and saw his mom and dad. He hugged his mother tightly and did not move until he felt safer and better. He thanked his dad for coming to his rescue and his friends Sid and Jugnu, who were smart to go to his parents to inform them that he had not come back from the jungle.

	Fox-F	Snake-S	Koala-K	Alpaca-A
Snake-S	SF	SS	SK	SA
Snake-S	SF	SS	SK	SA
Koala-K	KF	KS	KK	KA

164 Being a Mathematician

Tickle the Thoughts:

1. Ask the children how Guppy can change the scenario to get alpaca every time.
2. Ask them about the probability of Guppy meeting two snakes together in the jungle. Help them to check the places, which say SS in the Area Model. There are two such places.

$$SS = P \text{ (event)} \frac{\text{The combination that will make Guppy} \otimes}{\text{Total number of animals}} = \frac{2}{12}$$

$$SS = P \text{ (event)} \frac{\text{The combination of snake and snake}}{\text{Total number of animals}} = \frac{2}{12}$$

It can also be simplified to $\frac{1}{6}$

3. In case Sid was also lost in the jungle with Guppy, what was the probability of them meeting two alpacas? At no place on the Area Model does the 2AAs appear, therefore, the probability of Guppy and Sid meeting 2 alpacas =0/12

> **Goals Achieved**
> - Visualization of all the possible outcomes for a particular event or a probability scenario
> - Better conceptual understanding of the topic
> - Enhanced exploratory and hands on activities

Tick-tack Tips

1. To understand probability, you may choose to use jelly beans of different colours or different shapes.
2. You can use ideas that are more creative by using wool or

jute ropes to make the vertical and horizontal lines of the Probability Area Model.
3. The words used to represent probability in daily language are also chance, odds, may be, may be not, possibility, likelihood, etc.
4. The formula is simplified only for helping the children understand the concept.

Logical Learning Skills

Activity—35

Add with the Tic-Tac-Toe!

RESOURCES REQUIRED
- A4-sized papers
- A pen
- Building blocks

Getting Ready:

1. Keep building blocks with different numbers of 'bumps' on their heads.
2. The bumps should be between 1 and 9. One bump should represent number 1.
3. If you do not find a block with one bump, take two blocks with an even number of bumps and mount it over one another such that the total number of visible bumps on the two blocks combined add up to an odd number. Let us consider obtaining number 9. In the picture, the bigger red block has 8 bumps. Place the smaller red block, with two bumps, on the corner most bump of the bigger block. Therefore, the total number of visible bumps are 9 (8 + 2 =10; 10 − 1 [hidden bump] = 9).

170 Being a Mathematician

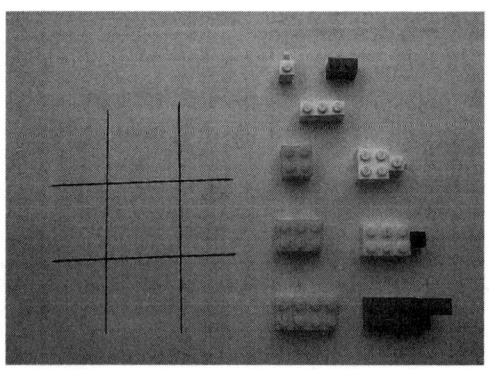

How to Play:

1. Invite a player to draw tic-tac-toe on an A4-sized paper as shown in the picture above.
2. Place the combinations of blocks such that each row or column in the tic-tac-toe must add up to 15. The children can add the numbers vertically, horizontally or diagonally. Do not place a block with 5 bumps at the centre of the tic-tac-toe. Give them only three turns to do so.

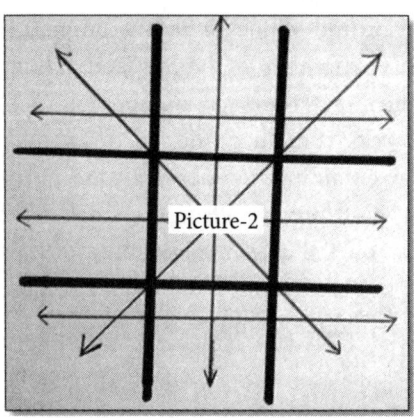

3. The player who gets the 15 correctly is the winner.

4. Let us understand the game with an example:
   - Gugzee and Jugnu are playing Tic-Tac-Toe. Gugzee goes first (G-1) and places the block with 8 bumps at the centre; next, Jugnu (J-2) places his blocks such that Gugzee is not able to make a 15. Therefore, he places one with 7 bumps on the right top corner (8 + 7= 15). However, this adds up to 15 without Gugzee playing her turn. So now, she must place a block (G-3) in any direction such that Jugnu is unable to add up to a total of 15. She places a block with 9 bumps on the top left corner arriving at 16 and 17 diagonally. From the limited number of blocks remaining, Jugnu decides to place (J-4), a block with 4 bumps, making the vertical total of 13 (9 + 4), and 17 (9 + 8) diagonally. Now, Gugzee (G-5) places a block with 2 bumps at the left corner to make the total 15 (9 + 4 + 2). Gugzee wins the game!

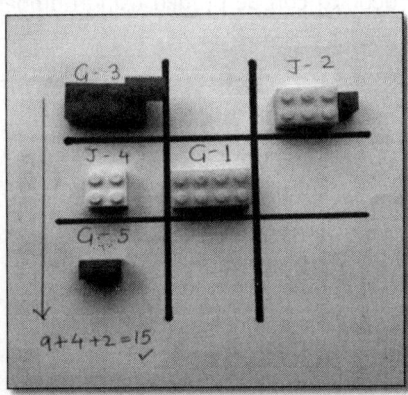

Tickle the Thoughts:

1. Ask the children why the first player should be barred from placing a block with 5 bumps at the centre of the Tic-Tac-Toe.

172 Being a Mathematician

2. Is there another winning number that they can use instead of 15?
3. Ask them the maximum total they can form using all the bumps on a block. Let them try it!

> **Goals Achieved**
> - Better concept of addition facts
> - Increased understanding of subtraction facts
> - Enhanced mental calculations
> - Promotes mathematical thinking

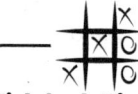

Tick-tack Tip

The same activity can be played using number flash cards instead of blocks.

Activity–36

Interesting Time Facts!

RESOURCES REQUIRED
- A notebook
- A paper and a pencil

Getting Ready:

Have a notebook of 200 pages ready with the page numbers marked.

How to Play:

1. Ask the children to choose a special occasion such as the upcoming birthday of their class teacher.
2. Now, ask them to calculate the seconds or minutes left for the birthday celebration to begin.
3. Ask the players to write down the facts on time.
4. Give them enough time to memorize these facts. Then, ask the children to hand over the sheet to you or cover them up to hide the answers.
5. Assign a number to each player and hand over a book of 200 pages to him or her.
6. Elect one player to keep the record of the points scored by each player.
7. Each player gets his or her turn to open the book and read the page number on the left. The number of the page the

player turns to will represent the number of seconds. Ask the children to make a note of the page numbers they turn to and add them up. The grand total of the pages will represent the seconds left for the party to begin.
8. If the child gets zero as the last number (such as page number 160) of the page, the player gets a chance to ask the other players a question based on 'time facts'.

Time Facts:

- A clock usually has two hands.
- The short hand is the hour hand.
- The long hand is the minute hand.
- 60 seconds = 1 minute
- 60 minutes = 1 hour
- 24 hours = 1 day (as per the convention)
- 23 hours, 56 minutes and 4.2 seconds = 1 day
- 7 days = 1 week
- 4 weeks = 1 month
- 12 months = 1 year
- 365 days (and 6 hours) = 1 year
- Leap year = 366 days
- 52 weeks = 1 year
- The hour hand takes 12 hours to complete one round of the clock.
- The hour hand of the clock does two full rounds in a day, i.e., $12 \times 2 = 24$ hours = 1 day.
- The minute hand takes 1 hour (60 minutes) to complete one round of the clock.
- The minute hand takes 60 seconds to complete 1 minute.
- Between any two numbers written on the clock are 5 minutes. (Multiples of 5!)

Activity-36

- Ante Meridiem, or A.M., is used for the first 12 hours of the day. It comes from a Latin word, meaning 'before midday'.
- Post Meridiem, or P.M., is used for the second 12 hours of the day, meaning 'after midday'.

Let us understand the different ways in which we can read the time:

Example:

Four o' clock or 4 p.m.

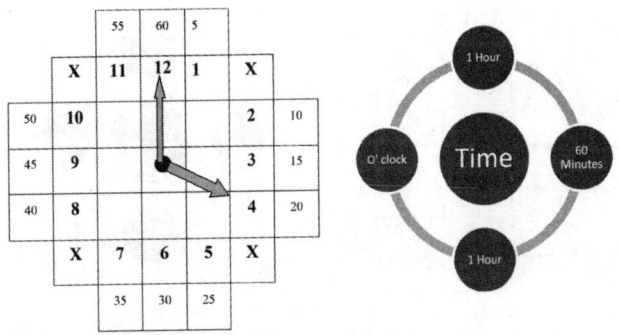

Quarter past four or 4:15 p.m.

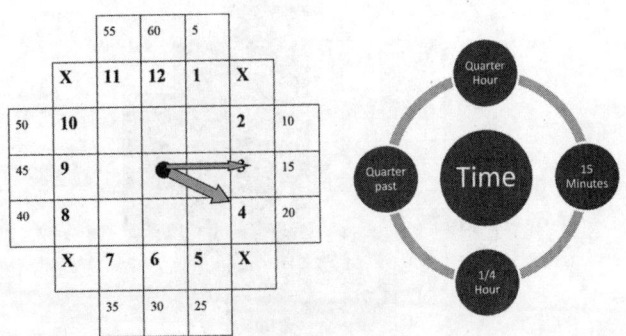

176 Being a Mathematician

Half past 4 or 4:30 p.m.

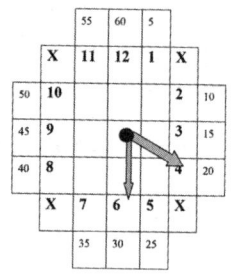 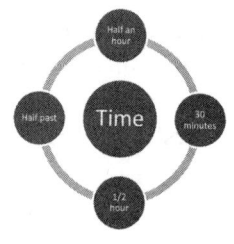

Quarter to 5 or 4:45 p.m.

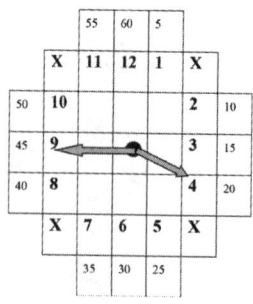 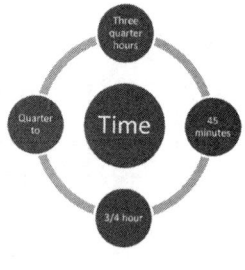

Left Side—To the (next) Hour   Right Side—Past the Hour

Activity-36   177

Ask the children to divide the clock into two vertical halves—the light (the left side) and dark (right side of the clock) sides of the clock.

If the minute hand is on the right (dark) side of the clock, it is 'past the hour'.

If the minute hand is on the left (light) side of the clock, it is 'to the (next) hour'.

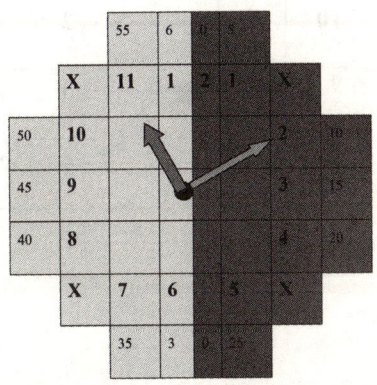

11:10
OR
10 minutes past 11.

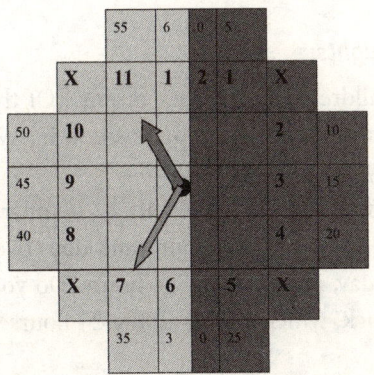

Being a Mathematician

11:35

OR

25 minutes to 12

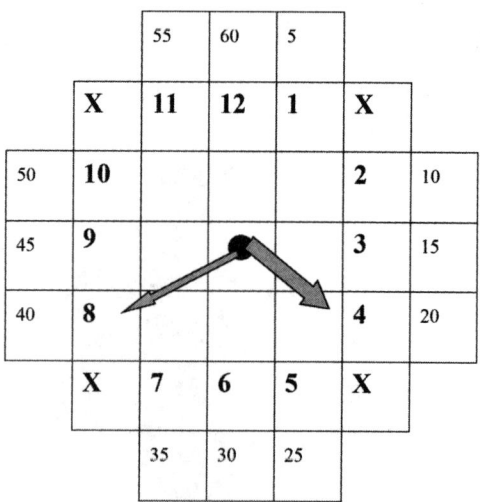

Any time before or after half hour can be read in three ways:
- 40 minutes past 4:00
- 4:40 p.m.
- 20 minutes to 5:00

Tickle the Thoughts:

1. Ask the children what *o' clock* means. (Of the clock)
2. Ask them to pick the right preposition in: What is the time of/in/on/by your watch?
3. Ask them why the clock has only 12 numbers when the day consists of 24 hours. The hour hand does two rounds of the clock in a day, i.e., 12 × 2 = 24 hours. Do you think we can create a clock, which shows all the 24 hours? Why and why not?

Activity-36

4. Ask them how they will write 'seven o' clock in the morning' in numbers. (7:00 a.m.)
5. Ask them how will they write 'seven o' clock in the evening' in numbers. (7:00 p.m.)
6. Ask them what is 'quarter' of 60 minutes.
7. Ask them 'time problems' such as: Sid goes to play football at 5:00 p.m. and comes back at 7:00 p.m. How long does he play football?

Solution:

	H	M
Time of departure from the football field =	7	00
Time of arrival at the football field =	− 5	00
Time spent on the field =	2	00

Sid played football for 2 hours.

- Jugnu's birthday party began at 6.00 p.m. and got over at 8.30 p.m. For how many hours did the party go on?

	H	M
Solution: Party got over =	8	30
Starting time =	− 6	00
The party went on for =	2	30

Jugnu's birthday party went on for 2 hours and 30 minutes.

Goals Achieved
- Better understanding of time facts
- Clearer concept of addition and subtraction of time
- Increased rote learning abilities
- Enhanced math language in the correct context

Tick-tack Tips

Share some interesting facts about time:

1. Time is used to measure the duration of events, intervals between them, and their sequence.
2. Despite what we've been taught, a day isn't a full 24 hours. It actually takes 23 hours, 56 minutes and 4.2 seconds for the earth to rotate once.
3. Just as it takes time for the children to leave home and reach the school, it takes time for sun's light to travel to earth, and as a result, when we see the sunlight, it has already travelled for the last 8 minutes and 20 seconds to reach us.
4. A single day on the planet Mercury is two Earth years long.
5. The earth's rotation is slowing, making the duration of a day slightly longer. In order to compensate for the lengthening days, the International Earth Rotation Service (the body which regulates astronomical time) periodically adds a second to the clock to keep things regular. This extra second is called a leap second. Before the first leap second was added in 1972, UTC (Universal Time Coordinated) was 10 seconds behind Atomic Time. So far, a total of 27 leap seconds have been added and the most recent leap second was added on 31 December 2016. Based on current predictions, the next leap second should be added on 30 June 2020.

Activity—37

Calendar Connections!

RESOURCES REQUIRED
- A calendar
- A paper and a pencil

Getting Ready:
1. Keep the calendar of the current year ready for reference.
2. A few calendar problem sums from 'Tickle the Thoughts' written beforehand.

Interesting Facts about Calendars:

There are seven days in a week:
1. Monday
2. Tuesday
3. Wednesday
4. Thursday
5. Friday
6. Saturday
7. Sunday
8. 52 weeks make 1 year
9. 4 weeks make 1 month
10. 12 months make 1 year
11. 365 days and 6 hours make 1 year

Being a Mathematician

12. Names of 12 months and the number of days

Months in a Year	Number of Days	Special Ocassions
January	31	
February	28/29	
March	31	
April	30	
May	31	
June	30	
July	31	
August	31	
September	30	
October	31	
November	30	
December	31	

How to Play:

1. Explain to the children how calendars are useful to us.
2. Help them mark the important dates on the calender such as his or her birthday and that of other family members.
3. Ask them to solve the calendar problem sums and give them the calendar as well. Allow them to flip the pages of the calendar and search for the answers.

Tickle the Thoughts:

Calendar problems:

- What is the date on the fourth Friday of March?
- What is the date on the third Saturday in the month of January?
- How many Sundays does February have?

Activity-37   183

- In which week of (name the month) is your birthday?
- In a year, how many days go by before your birthday? For example, the child's birthday is on the 2nd of February, then the answer is 31 days of the month of January and 2 more days of February (31 + 2= 33). The child's birthday is on the 33rd day of the year!
-

🎯 Goals Achieved
- Better understanding of the calendar word problems
- Enhanced number relationships
- Increased math vocabulary related to date/time and measurement

Tick-tack Tips
1. Help them understand seasons in a year.
2. Share information with the children about the rotation and the revolution of the earth.
3. Share information about the Sundial Jantar Mantar.

Activity—38

Subtraction with Calendar Rings!

> ### RESOURCES REQUIRED
> - A calendar
> - Newspapers
> - 3 chart papers
> - A pair of child-safe scissors
> - A glue

Getting Ready:

Keep the required resources ready.

Method to Make the 'Number Line':

1. Ask the children to take three chart papers and stick them length-wise such that it accommodates 31 (days of the month) rings.
2. Now help the children think of a special occasion and count the number of days remaining. Let us consider that the present day is the 1st of the month and the child's birthday is on 31st of the same month.
3. Draw a giant number line on the chart paper and mark the numbers, starting from 1 to 31, at equal distances.
4. Next, either place the giant number line vertically on the wall or place it on the floor.

5. The display of the rings next to the number line will help the children understand the progression of days.

Method to Make the Rings:

1. Ask the children to take the newspaper and using the child-safe scissors, cut 31 to 35 (a few extra strips just in case a few get spoilt) 6"-long and 1"-wide strips. Ask the children to write corresponding numbers starting from 1 to 31 on each strip to represent the dates of the month.
2. Next, ask them to stick the two ends of a strip to make it into a 'ring'. Then pass another strip through the ring and stick its ends to make a chain of rings.

How to Play:

1. Ask the children to place the rings over the number line and count the number of days until their birthday or the special occasion.
2. Each day, ask the children to remove 1 ring from the chain. Ask them to subtract the present date with the birthday date. For example, if the child has untied the 29th ring, ask him or her to subtract it from 31 (in this example 31st represents the birthday of the child) 31 − 29=?
3. Encourage them to do the subtraction sums for other players, too. This way, children will have more number of sums to solve.

Tickle the Thoughts:

1. Ask them how many number of days have gone by and how many are remaining. For example, 30 days have gone by and only one day is remaining before the birthday party.
2. What was the date yesterday, today and what will be the date tomorrow?

186 Being a Mathematician

3. How many days were there for their birthday last Monday?
4. Have they crossed the middle mark? Can they represent the middle mark on the number line?
5. If they have 10 days until their birthday, how many did they have yesterday? How many days will they have tomorrow?

Goals Achieved
- Improved mental math
- Increased understanding about the number relationships
- Increased understanding about the addition facts and subtraction facts
- Better understanding of the concept of calendar

Tick-tack Tips
1. To reduce the level of complexity of the game, use a calendar for reference to point out the dates to the children.
2. Also, you may place sticky notes next to each ring facing front.
3. If the children are doing this activity at school, then they may mark the weekends with some glitter, as they will not be in school to take the rings off for those days.

Activity—39

Finding the Leap Year!

RESOURCES REQUIRED
- Paper and a pencil
- Old calendars
- 1 toothpick
- A ball
- 2-metres-long wool
- A large bead

Getting Ready:

Keep the calendars of the past 10 years ready for reference. Keep a bead, with holes large enough for a toothpick to pass through it, ready, to show them the rotation of the earth around its axis.

Some Interesting Facts:

Earth's revolution around the sun:
1. Explain to them that it takes one day for the earth to rotate on its axis while it revolves around the sun in its orbit. Use the bead to represent the earth, the toothpick to represent the imaginary axis of the earth and the ball (preferably yellow) to represent the sun.
2. Place the wool around the ball (sun) to form an elliptical path to represent the earth's orbit.

3. Inform the children that it takes a year for the earth to complete one revolution around the sun. It reaches the same point in its orbit from where it had begun. So, after every 365 days and 6 hours, the earth reaches the same point in its orbit from where it began.
4. Since a year has exactly 365 days and 6 hours, to keep the approximations convenient, the 6 hours are compounded 4 times in 4 years to make 1 day (6+6+6+6=24 hours=1 day) We add this extra day to every fourth year and call it a leap year. And of course, this year has 366 days.

How to Find Leap Years:

Here is how the children can distinguish between a leap year and a non-leap year.

Leap Years	Non-leap Years
• The year is divisible by 4, i.e., leaving no remainder. For example, 1904 divided by 4 gives 476.0. • This year has 366 days.	• The year is not divisible by 4, i.e. it leaves a remainder. For example, 1883 divided by 4 gives 470.75. • This year has 365 days and 6 hours.

Years that have two zeros at their ends, such as 500, 600, 1900, etc., are called century years.

How to Identify Century Years

Century Leap Years	Century Non-leap Years
• Divide the century year by 400. Century leap years are divisible by 400—does not leave a remainder. For example, 2000 divided by 400 leaves no remainder.	• Divide the century year by 400. Century non-leap years will not be divisible by 400 and will leave a remainder that is not zero. For example, 1900 divided by 400 gives 4.75

Activity—39

Tickle the Thoughts:

1. Ask the children if they were born in a leap year.
2. Ask them to find out if their friend's/parent's/teacher's birth year is a leap year.

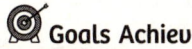 **Goals Achieved**
- Better concept building abilities
- Increased understanding of division properties

Tick-tack Tip
Share information about the rotation of the earth on its axis and the concept of day and night by using a source of light, such as a torch, to show the rising of sun and the beginning of a day.

Activity—40

Balance!

RESOURCES REQUIRED

The Balance:
- An old cloth hanger
- A jute rope
- 2 identical paper cups
- Hole punch
- A pair of child-safe scissors
- Things to measure with: cotton, wool, pebbles, flour, rice, etc.
- Paper and pencils

Getting Ready:

Make a list of things to be measured in the surroundings.

Method:

1. Ask the children to choose two identical paper cups to make the buckets of the balance.
2. Ask them to punch holes, using the hole punch, on the opposite sides of each cup close to the brim.
3. Now ask them to take the child-safe scissors and cut two-equal size jute ropes/ribbons of 50 cm each.
4. Next, ask them to take a rope/ribbon, pass it through the punched holes and tie a knot at the end of the rope next to

Activity-40   191

the brim of the cup. Then, pass the other end of the rope through the other hole of the cup to make the loop of a bucket.
5. Repeat the process for the second cup too.
6. Lastly, ask the children to hang the buckets at point 'B' and 'C' of the hanger. Refer to the given picture. The balance is ready for measuring.

How to Play:

1. Offer different items to the children and ask them to guess what will happen if they place the items in the two buckets?

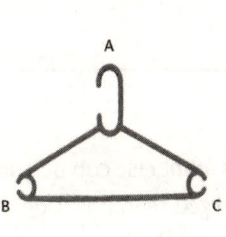

2. Ask the children to put different or same items in the buckets and hold the balance from the point 'A'. Else, children may also hang the balance from a doorknob.
3. Allow the balance to stabilize.
4. Now, ask the children to write the names of the items on the paper and record their observations.

Tickle the Thoughts:

1. Ask them why they think the buckets are/are not at the same level.

2. Ask them which item they think is heavier and why.
3. Ask them if they weigh the sand first, and then, add water to it and weigh it again, will it still weigh the same and why and why not.

Goals Achieved
- Better understanding of the concept of estimation
- Better understanding of the concept of mass
- Promotes data-handling abilities
- Clearer concept of sorting, ordering, comparing and classifying

Tick-tack Tips
1. Encourage the children to think what else can be added to the balance to give more standardized readings. Can a 'pointer' be added to the balance to indicate the exact readings? How?
2. Introduce them to the different types of balance and share information regarding the properties of different materials.
3. Encourage the children to compare the recorded data, sort out the items having the same weight, classify the data obtained in the increasing order of weight.

Conclusion

The world is evolving at a very fast pace, and we need to keep abreast with the changing trends. The challenges we experience are not those that our succeeding generations are going to encounter. However, without knowing the challenges the future is going to bring in, it becomes imperative for the educators to make their teachings 'timeless'.

It is time for us to help the emerging generation to overcome all barriers and fears of learning, and aim for more distinguished achievements in life. This can only be achieved when we help children with developing the 'required thinking' for understanding the subject rather than focussing on the subject to get scores. Scores have done a lot of damage to the confidence and self-esteem of a child than adding to his or her personality. And Mathematics tops the list of subjects for a majority of students who fail to score well in it and get a pat on their shoulders for their performance. However, if we refocus to use Mathematics as a tool to develop mathematical thinking, the primary goal of achieving deeper and more profound knowledge is achieved for the child. The paramount importance given to academic scores should shift to enhancing the depth of knowledge of a child during the learning process. The true comparison should be between previous knowledge and the development shown by the child, rather than in comparison with another child's performance.

Teach the children to disregard superfluous scores, undue appreciation and painful labels in life. Enlighten them to look at the deeper, more profound and pleasant aspects of learning. The knowledge we impart to the future generations should empower them to create an inclusive world worth living for every child. Let us celebrate profound learning!

Acknowledgements

I thank my immediate family for stepping in and standing in for me while I would constructively engage myself and put pen to paper.

Writing a book is harder than I typically thought and more rewarding than I could have ever imagined. None of this would have been possible without my friends; I thank them for providing a constant source of strength.

I'm forever indebted to Ms Yamini Chowdhury for her editorial help, keen insight and ongoing support in thoughtfully bringing my ultimate dreams to life.

My sincere thanks to Saswati Bora for willingly giving her inputs, Anurupa Sen for editing, Raj Kumari for typesetting and Amrita for intelligently designing the attractive cover of this book, and everybody at Rupa Publications for typically investing considerable time and collaborative effort in shaping the published book to its present form.

To gratefully acknowledge is to admirably express my sincere gratitude to all of you who undoubtedly remain an integral part of my extraordinary journey.

It is for you that this book became a reality.